Charles W. S. Williams
A Checklist

Charles W. S. Williams

A Checklist

Lois Glenn

The Kent State University Press

The Serif Series: Number 33
Bibliographies and Checklists
Dean H. Keller, General Editor
Kent State University

Library of Congress Cataloging in Publication Data
Glenn, Lois.
    Charles W. S. Williams.
    (The Serif series : bibliographies and checklists ; no. 33)
    Includes indexes.
    1. Williams, Charles, 1886-1945—Bibliography.
I. Series.
Z8976.3.G56   [PR6045.I5]   016.828'9'1209   75-17277
ISBN 0-87338-179-3

Contents

Introduction

In the mythic revival of the 1960s, Charles Williams's seven novels appeared, along with J. R. R. Tolkien's *Lord of the Rings* and C. S. Lewis's planetary trilogy, in paperback editions, becoming for the first time readily accessible to American readers. Although the Williams novels did not achieve the popular success of the Tolkien works, Williams is assured the long-term attention of scholars because of his influence on T. S. Eliot, W. H. Auden, and C. S. Lewis.

For Eliot, Williams the man approached the saintly, and Williams the writer was a source for images and characters. Although Williams probably considered his Arthurian cycle of poems artistically more serious than his novels, it was the novels and theological writings, not the poetry, that had the greatest impact on poets like Eliot and Auden. Complex, obscure themes, such as the bearing of another's burdens and approaching God through the affirmative and negative ways of life, occur in the Arthurian poems, but they are introduced in simpler form and explained in his theological works (*He Came Down from Heaven* and *Forgiveness of Sins*). Even his literary criticism—especially his *Figure of Beatrice*—depends on themes that recur in his canon. Indeed, his use of theme was perhaps his most significant contribution to a lasting literature.

One of the most prolific writers of his time, Williams published seven novels, seven volumes of poetry, fifteen plays, four books of criticism, four prose works on religious subjects, six biographies, many articles for British periodicals, and over two hundred reviews. An editor for Oxford University Press (Amen House), Williams managed to lecture to night classes in London and meet C. S. Lewis, J. R. R. Tolkien, and other writers for weekly readings of works in progress.

No previous checklist gives complete and correct information about Williams's published works. Anne Ridler's *Image of the City* (a collection of Williams's essays) and Mary McDermott Shideler's *Theology of Romantic Love* (the best of the critical works on Williams) contain helpful but incomplete lists of Williams's published works. This checklist offers students and scholars a complete list (in order of publication) of Williams's published writings in all genres. Publication information for his books includes first and successive editions, along with dates of reprints. The note accompanying each entry suggests the nature of the work. A list of secondary materials includes major works about Williams and his work, as well as others that merely mention him. The annotations for secondary materials are guides for reading, not summaries.

The University of Texas at Austin has an excellent collection of first editions of Williams's books, including a number of signed copies. I found this collection (housed in the Harry Ransom Center) more complete than any other single library collection, including that at the British Museum.

I. Williams's Works

A. Books

i. Poetry

1. *The Silver Stair*. London: Herbert and Daniel, 1912. 90 pp.

   Alice and Wilfrid Meynell paid the publication costs for this volume of poetry. The sonnet series treats romantic love in the Dantean sense.

2. *Poems of Conformity*. London: Oxford University Press, 1917. 127 pp.

   Love and marriage in the Way of Affirmation are the dominant themes.

3. *Divorce*. London: Oxford University Press, 1920. 120 pp.

   The poems of this volume are concerned with war, love, death, religion, the City, and the Way of Affirmation.

4. *Windows of Night*. London: Oxford University Press, 1924. 152 pp.

   These poems explore the dark sides of religion and love.

5. *Heroes and Kings*. London: Sylvan Press, 1930. 76 pp.

   The primary theme of the poems is love.

6. *Taliessin through Logres*. London: Oxford University Press, 1938. 96 pp.

   The lyric cycle has as its theme the Matter of Britain,

involving the reign of King Arthur and the achievement of
the Grail. To give emphasis to the symbol of the Grail,
Williams reworks the traditional material and
employs a complex symbolism, which is somewhat
obscure. Williams's major themes appear. See combined
edition (I-A-i-8). Sixteen of the poems are reprinted
in *Selected Writings* (I-A-iv-7).

7. *The Region of the Summer Stars*. London: PL, Editions
   Poetry London, Nicholson and Watson, 1944,
   55 pp.; London: Oxford University Press,
   1950, rpt. 1952, 1960, 1969, 61 pp.

   Williams considered these eight poems incidental to
   the main theme treated in *Taliessin through Logres* (I-A-i-6),
   yet they are a part of the Arthurian cycle and are
   treated as such by C. S. Lewis in *Arthurian Torso* (I-A-iv-5).
   See combined edition (I-A-i-8). Five of these poems
   are reprinted in *Selected Writings* (I-A-iv-7).

8. *Taliessin through Logres and The Region of the Summer
   Stars*. London: Oxford University Press,
   1954, rpt. 1960. 96 pp, 61 pp.

   For annotations see separate titles (I-A-i-6, 7).

ii. Novels

1. *War in Heaven*. London: Victor Gollancz, 1930,
   288 pp.; London: Faber and Faber, 1947, rpt. 1962,
   256 pp.; New York: Pellegrini and Cudahy,
   1949, 290 pp.; Grand Rapids, Michigan:
   William B. Eerdmans, 1965, 256 pp.

   A struggle over the Grail polarizes forces of self-interest
   and self-denial. Themes introduced in this novel
   recur in the other six.

2. *Many Dimensions.* London: Victor Gollancz, 1931,
   317 pp.; London: Faber and Faber, 1947,
   rpt. 1963, 269 pp.; New York: Pellegrini and
   Cudahy, 1949, 308 pp.; Harmondsworth,
   England: Penguin Books, 1952, 254 pp.; Grand
   Rapids, Michigan: William B. Eerdmans,
   1965, 269 pp.

   The magical stone of the Crown of Suleiman arouses
   acquisitiveness in a number of power-seekers. As in the other
   novels, the conflict between the forces of good and
   evil is dominant.

3. *The Place of the Lion.* London: Mundanus (V.
   Gollancz), 1931, 288 pp., reissued in 1947, 175 pp.;
   New York: W. W. Norton, 1932, 288 pp.;
   New York: Pellegrini and Cudahy, 1951, 236
   pp.; London: Faber and Faber, 1952, rpt.
   1965, 206 pp.; Grand Rapids, Michigan: William
   B. Eerdmans, 1965, 206 pp.

   In this novel the release of archetypal beasts into this
   world causes confusion and terror and ultimately
   distinguishes the selfish from the unselfish, the evil from
   the good.

4. *The Greater Trumps.* London: Victor Gollancz, 1932,
   287 pp.; New York: Pellegrini and Cudahy,
   1950, 268 pp.; London: Faber and Faber, 1954,
   rpt. 1964, 230 pp.; New York: Noonday Press, 1950,
   rpt. 1962, 268 pp.

   The original Tarot pack arouses desires for godlike
   powers in two men who are opposed by those who resist
   the perversion of a sacred object. The themes of substitution
   and exchange emerge in this novel but are not clearly
   defined.

5. *Shadows of Ecstasy.* London: Victor Gollancz, 1933,
   287 pp.; London: Faber and Faber, 1948, rpt.
   1965, 224 pp.; New York: Pellegrini and
   Cudahy, 1950, 260 pp.; Grand Rapids, Michigan:
   William B. Eerdmans, 1965, 224 pp.

   Williams wrote this novel first and published it later.
   It concerns a revolution in Africa led by a man who claims
   ascendancy over death.

6. *Descent into Hell.* London: Faber and Faber, 1937,
   305 pp., reissued in 1949, rpt. 1955, 1961,
   222 pp.; New York: Pellegrini and Cudahy, 1949,
   248 pp.; Grand Rapids, Michigan: William
   B. Eerdmans, 1965, 222 pp.

   Considered by many to be Williams's best novel,
   Descent into Hell involves the intensification of self or of
   self-denial, the one leading to complete introversion,
   the other to substitution and exchange.

7. *All Hallows' Eve.* London: Faber and Faber, 1945,
   206 pp., reissued in 1947, rpt. 1960, 1966,
   240 pp. [includes an introduction by T. S. Eliot];
   New York: Noonday Press, 1963, 273 pp.
   [includes the Eliot introduction].

   Although a magician is able to gain followers and power
   by means of sorcery, those practicing exchange
   ultimately defeat him. This is the last of the novels to be
   published.

iii. Plays

1. *The Masque of the Manuscript,* written by Charles
   Williams and set to music by Hubert J. Foss.
   London: privately printed by Henderson
   and Spaulding, 1927. 18 pp.

   Staged on April 28, the masque follows the publication
   process of a manuscript.

2. *A Myth of Shakespeare.* London: Oxford University Press, 1928, rpt. 1929, reissued in the Oxford Bookshelf, 1936. 146 pp.

   This blank-verse drama was composed for an evening class.

3. *The Masque of Perusal,* written by Charles Williams and set to music by Hubert J. Foss. London: privately printed by Henderson and Spaulding, 1929, 24 pp.

   This masque is about the manuscript in *The Masque of the Manuscript* (I-A-iii-1) after it is published.

4. *Three Plays.* London: Oxford University Press, 1931. 200 pp.

   The Witch, preceded by "Taliessin's Song of Logres," presents the death of love through waste. *The Chaste Wanton,* preceded by "Taliessin's Song of Byzantium," portrays the death of love by its own consent. *The Rite of the Passion,* preceded by "Taliessin's Song of the King's Crowning" and followed by "Taliessin's Song of the Setting of Galahad in the King's Bed," was written for Good Friday (1929) for Henry Lee, Vicar of St. Martin's. It presents the Christian story of the death of Love to renew love in humanity. The end piece is "Epilogue in Somerset: A Song of the Myths."

5. *Thomas Cranmer of Canterbury.* London: Oxford University Press, 1936, 75 pp.; [*Cranmer of Canterbury: Acting Edition for the Festival of the Friends of Canterbury Cathedral*] Canterbury: H. J. Goulden, 1936, 42 pp.; [*Four Modern Verse Plays,* ed. Elliott M. Browne] Harmondsworth: Penguin Books, 1957, pp. 143-200.

   For annotation see *Collected Plays* (I-A-iii-9).

6. *Judgement at Chelmsford: A Pageant Play Written . . . for Performance at the New Scala Theatre London . . . in Celebration of the Twenty-fifth Anniversary of the*

Diocese of Chelmsford. London: Oxford
University Press, 1939. 93 pp.

For annotation see *Collected Plays* (I-A-iii-9).

7. *The House of the Octopus.* London: Edinburgh House
Press, 1945. 115 pp.

For annotation see *Collected Plays* (I-A-iii-9).

8. *Seed of Adam and Other Plays.* London: Oxford
University Press, 1948. 95 pp.

The contents are *Seed of Adam, The Death of Good
Fortune, The House by the Stable,* and *Grab and Grace.* For
annotation see *Collected Plays* (I-A-iii-9). *The House by the Stable*
and *Grab and Grace* were reprinted in *Religious Drama,*
3 (1959), 29-78. *The Seed of Adam* was reprinted in
Selected Writings (I-A-iv-7).

9. *Collected Plays by Charles Williams,* ed. John
Heath-Stubbs. London: Oxford University
Press, 1963. 401 pp.

Nine plays are included:

Thomas Cranmer of Canterbury, commissioned for the Canterbury Festival
of 1935, involves the martyrdom of Cranmer in relation to the
conflicts of the times.

Judgement at Chelmsford . . . portrays a history of the diocese and of the
soul's journey to the City of God.

Seed of Adam, written for the drama society of Chelmsford Diocese and
produced in 1936, involves Adam's attempts to return to God and
Paradise; Williams's distortions of time are of some interest here.

The Death of Good Fortune: A Christmas Play was Williams's last finished
stage play, portraying Good Fortune's discovery of his own redemption by Christ.

The House by the Stable: A Christmas Play involves a struggle for Man's
soul.

Grab and Grace: It's the Second Step, companion and sequel to the pre-
ceding play, continues the story of the soul's progress toward
grace.

House of the Octopus, written for the United Council for Missionary
  Education, revolves around a struggle between the forces of
  P'o-l'u (Hell) and those of Heaven.
Terror of Light, the only one of the plays in prose, takes place after the
  Resurrection as the disciples plan for their futures and discover
  the principle of exchange.
The Three Temptations was written for a broadcast done in November
  1942. Distorting time, Williams treats the life of Christ.

iv. Criticism

1. *Poetry at Present.* Oxford: Clarendon Press, 1930;
   Freeport, New York: Books for Libraries Press, 1969.
   216 pp.

   Included are essays on Thomas Hardy, Robert Bridges,
   A. E. Housman, Rudyard Kipling, W. B. Yeats, W. H. Davies,
   Walter de la Mare, G. K. Chesterton, John Masefield,
   Ralph Hodgson, Wilfrid Gibson, Lascelles Abercrombie,
   T. S. Eliot, Edith, Osbert and Sacheverell Sitwell,
   Robert Graves and Edmund Blunden, and sixteen of his own
   poems—a prelude and fifteen end pieces.

2. *The English Poetic Mind.* Oxford: Clarendon Press,
   1932; New York: Russell and Russell,
   1963. 213 pp.

   The substance of the work was delivered as a special course
   for the City Literary Institute at the London Day
   Training College in 1931. A particular kind of crisis which
   he recognizes in the works of Shakespeare, Wordsworth and
   other British poets is the thesis. "Note on Great
   Poetry," "The Growth of a Poet's Mind," "Milton" and
   "Wordsworth" are reprinted in *Selected Writings* (I-A-iv-7).

3. *Reason and Beauty in the Poetic Mind.* Oxford:
   Clarendon Press, 1933. 186 pp.

   Williams discusses reason in Wordsworth's *Prelude*, the

abandonment of intellect by Keats in two odes,
reason in *Paradise Lost* and in Shakespeare's tragedies.
Also he explores the concept of beauty in Marlowe's
Tamburlaine, Keats's odes, *Paradise Lost*, and Shakespeare's
Troilus and *Othello*.

4. *The Figure of Beatrice*. London: Faber and Faber,
   1943, rpt. 1944, 1946, 1950, 1958; New
   York: Noonday Press, 1961. 236 pp.

   Williams examines the expression of the Way of
   Affirmation in the poetry of Dante. This work reveals
   Williams's criticism at its best.

5. "The Figure of Arthur," *Arthurian Torso: Containing
   the Posthumous Fragment of* The Figure of Arthur
   *by Charles Williams and a Commentary on the
   Arthurian Poems of Charles Williams* by C. S. Lewis.
   London: Oxford University Press, 1948,
   rpt. 1952, 1969. 199 pp.

   The unfinished piece is a history of and commentary on
   the Arthurian legend and should be considered
   a companion piece to Williams's lyric cycle. The first
   two chapters were read to J. R. R. Tolkien and C. S.
   Lewis, who in 1945 gave a series of lectures on
   Williams's Arthurian cycle. "What Then Is the Achievement
   of the Grail" is reprinted in *Selected Writings* (I-A-iv-7).

6. *The Image of the City and Other Essays*, ed. Anne
   Ridler. London: Oxford University Press, 1958.
   199 pp.

   Included are more than forty essays and short pieces by
   Williams on various subjects. "The Cross,"
   "Natural Goodness," "The Index of the Body," "The Way
   of Exchange," "The Way of Affirmation," and
   "Malory and the Grail Legend" were reprinted in *Selected
   Writings* (I-A-iv-7).

7. *Selected Writings*, ed. Anne Ridler. Oxford
   Paperbacks, No. 21. London: Oxford University
   Press, 1961. 244 pp.

   Contains reprints of Williams's prose, poetry and drama.

v. Theology

1. *He Came Down from Heaven*. I Believe Series, No. 5.
   London: Heinemann, 1938. 147 pp.

   An important work, this volume contains an explanation
   of Williams's theological position concerning the
   fall of man, sin, redemption and substituted
   love. See combined edition (I-A-v-5).

2. *The Descent of the Dove: A Short History of the Holy
   Spirit in the Church*. London: Longmans,
   Green, 1939, 245 pp.; New York: Oxford
   University Press, 1939, 245 pp.; London: Faber
   and Faber, 1950, rpt. 1955, 1963, 245
   pp.; New York: Pellegrini and Cudahy, 1950,
   245 pp.; New York: Meridian Books,
   1956, 240 pp. [includes an introduction by
   W. H. Auden]; London: Collins, Fontana Library,
   1963, 224 pp.; Grand Rapids, Michigan:
   William B. Eerdmans, 1965, 245 pp.

   Williams explores the paradox "This also is Thou; neither
   is this Thou" as an appropriate summary of the
   history of the Christian Church.

3. *Witchcraft*. London: Faber and Faber, 1941;
   Cleveland: World Publishing, 1959.
   316 pp.

   Williams discusses the development of the idea of the
   devil and the activities associated with witchcraft
   in Christian times.

4. *The Forgiveness of Sins*. London: G. Bles, 1942.
   123 pp.

   Dedicated to the Inklings, the volume treats forgiveness as
   it appears in Shakespeare and in Christian theology
   and suggests how it should operate among
   men. See combined edition (I-A-v-5).

5. *He Came Down from Heaven and The Forgiveness of Sins*. London: Faber and Faber, 1950, rpt. 1956. 200 pp.

For annotations see separate titles (I-A-v-1, 4).

vi. Biographies

1. *Bacon*. London: Arthur Barker, 1933; New York: Harper and Brothers, 1934; Folcroft, Pennsylvania: Folcroft Library, 1973. 318 pp.

   Williams wrote "Myth of Francis Bacon" in verse at the request of Olive Willis for presentation at Downe House in July 1932. Finding no modern biography of Bacon, Williams decided to write one.

2. *James I*. London: Arthur Barker, 1934, 1951; New York: Roy Publishers, 1953 [an introduction by Dorothy L. Sayers appears in the 1951 and 1953 editions]; Freeport, New York: Books for Libraries Press, 1969. 310 pp.

   Williams treats both the absurdity and potentiality of his character.

3. *Rochester*. London: Arthur Barker, 1935. 274 pp.

   Williams sees Rochester as a romantic, who adopts the contemporary attitude of fidelity to sensation rather than to imagination. The treatment ends with Rochester's conversion to faith.

4. *Queen Elizabeth*. Great Lives Series. London: Duckworth, 1936, reissued as *Queen Elizabeth I*, 1953. 143 pp.

   Williams treats the queen and her period.

5. *Henry VII*. London: Arthur Barker, 1937. 272 pp.

   Williams is particularly concerned with Henry's quiet but effective establishment of power and reorganization of the monarchy.

6. *Stories of Great Names.* London: Oxford University Press, 1937. 216 pp.

Included are biographical sketches of Alexander, Julius Caesar, Charlemagne, Joan of Arc, Shakespeare, Voltaire and Wesley.

7. *Flecker of Dean Close.* London: Canterbury Press, 1946. 94 pp.

The headmaster of Dean Close School and the Victorian age are the subjects of this work.

B. Poems and Stories

1. "Scene from a Mystery." *New Witness*, 15 (December 12, 1919), 70-73.

   A play.

2. "Briseis." *A Miscellany of British Poetry, 1919.* Ed. W. Kean Seymour. London: Cecil Palmer and Hayward, 1919; New York: Harcourt, Brace and Howe, 1919. P. 145.

3. "Christmas." *A Miscellany of British Poetry, 1919.* Ed. W. Kean Seymour. London: Cecil Palmer and Hayward, 1919; New York: Harcourt, Brace and Howe, 1919. Pp. 142-44.

4. "Absence." *London Mercury*, 5 (March 1922), 462.

   An early poem.

5. "The Moon." London: Oxford University Press Music Department, 1923; London: Faber and Faber, 1947. 28 pp.

   Williams wrote the words for the cantata prepared by W. Gillies Whittaker from Henry Purcell's work.

6. "Beauty Lately." London: Oxford University Press Music Department, 1925. 5 leaves.

   English words by Williams for music by G. F. Handel. Arranged and edited by W. G. Whittaker.

7. "Stabat Mater Dolorosa." London: Oxford University Press Music Department, 1926. 56 pp.

   This is a translation of a medieval Latin hymn.

8. *An Urbanity*. London: privately printed by
   Henderson and Spaulding, 1927.

   The characters of the masques appear in this work,
   written especially for the actors in the Amen
   House masques.

9. "The Carol of Amen House," words by Charles
   Williams, music by Hubert J. Foss. London:
   privately printed by Henderson and Spaulding, 1927.
   6 leaves.

10. "To Music." *Dominant*, 1 (June 1928), 40.

    A poem.

11. "Percivale's Song." *New English Poems: A
    Miscellany of Contemporary Verse Never Before Published.*
    Collected by Lascelles Abercrombie.
    London: V. Gollancz, 1931. Pp. 345-46.

12. "Taliessin's Song of Lancelot's Mass." *New
    English Poems: A Miscellany of Contemporary Verse Never
    Before Published.* Collected by Lascelles
    Abercrombie. London: V. Gollancz, 1931.
    Pp. 340-44.

13. "Cressida." *Modern Poetry, 1922-1934: An Anthology.*
    Comp. Maurice Wollman. London: Macmillan,
    1934. P. 12.

14. "Et in Sempiternum Pereant." *London Mercury*,
    33 (December 1935), 151-58.

    This short story concerns a character from *Many Dimensions*
    (I-A-ii-1).

15. "Prelude," "Taliessin's Return to Logres,"
    "The Vision of Empire," "The Calling of

Arthur." *Christendom* (A Journal of Christian Sociology), 8 (March 1938), 19-30.

These are early versions of poems from the *Taliessin* cycle.

16. "The Periodical." *Periodical*, 24 (July 1939), 77.

    A poem.

17. "Divites Dimisit." *Theology*, 39 (December 1939), 421-24.

    An early version of the poem "The Prayers of the Pope."

18. "Apologue on the Parable of the Wedding Garment." *Time and Tide*, 21 (December 7, 1940), 1186.

    A poem, reprinted in *Image* (I-A-iv-6), pp. 166-68.

19. "The Coming of Palomides." *Modern Verse 1900-1950*. Ed. Phyllis M. Jones. World's Classics. London: Oxford University Press, 1940, rpt. 1941, 1942, 1943, new edition 1955, rpt. 1957, 1959, 1962, 1965, 1969, 1972. Pp. 122-27.

20. "Taliessin in the Rose Garden." *Dublin Review*, 208 (January 1941), 82-86.

    The version is different from the one appearing in *Taliessin through Logres* (I-A-i-6).

21. "Dinadan's Song." *Time and Tide*, 22 (March 15, 1941), 210.

    A poem.

22. "On the Sanctissimum: with an Epilogue." *Theology*, 43 (September 1941), 141-44.

    Poems.

23. "For a Musician's Birthday Book." *Time and Tide*, 22 (November 29, 1941), 1038.

    A poem.

24. "The Queen's Servant." *Poetry London*, 2 (1942-1943),
    38-41.

    A poem from the final *Taliessin* cycle.

25. "To Michal: After Marriage," The Grasshopper
    Broadsheets. Third series, number 10.
    London: Kenneth Hopkins, 1944. 1 leaf.

26. "The Calling of Arthur." *Penguin Anthology of
    Contemporary Verse*. Ed. Kenneth Allot.
    Harmondsworth, England: Penguin, 1950.
    Pp. 73-74.

    Poem from the *Taliessin* cycle.

27. "Mount Badon," and "Taliessin's Song of the
    Unicorn," *The Faber Book of Twentieth
    Century Verse*. Revised edition. Ed. John
    Heath-Stubbs and David Wright. London:
    Faber and Faber, 1953, 1965, 1967, rpt. 1970.
    Pp. 336-38, 338-39.

    Poem from the *Taliessin* cycle.

28. "The Noises That Weren't There: Chapter I,"
    Mythlore, 2 (Autumn 1970), 17-21; "The Voice of the
    Rat: Chapter II," *Mythlore*, 2 (Winter 1971),
    17-23; Untitled, "Chapter III," *Mythlore*, 2
    (Winter 1972), 21-25.

    An unfinished fiction manuscript.

29. "To Michal: Sonnets after Marriage," *Mythlore*,
    2 (Autumn 1970), 5.

    A poem reprinted from *Windows of Night* (I-A-i-4).

30. "Ballade of a Street Door." *Mythlore*, 2
    (Winter 1971), 18.

    A poem.

C. Articles and Letters

1. "The Hero in English Verse." *Contemporary Review*, 118 (December 1920), 831-38.

   A study of the heroes' struggles and the way each managed to triumph.

2. "The Commonwealth in English Verse." *Contemporary Review*, 124 (August 1923), 228-36.

3. "Note on Possible Endings to Edwin Drood." *The Mystery of Edwin Drood* by Charles Dickens. World's Classics Series. London: Oxford University Press, 1924. Pp. 366-76.

4. "Prefatory Note." *A Book of Longer Modern Verse*. Selected by Edward A. Parker. Oxford: Clarendon Press, 1926. P. vii.

5. "The One-eared Man." *Dominant*, 1 (December 1927), 11-12.

6. "Preface." *A Book of Victorian Narrative Verse*. Chosen by Charles Williams. Oxford: Clarendon Press, 1927, rpt. 1931. Pp. iii-x.

   Reprinted in *Image* (I-A-iv-6), pp. 1-6.

7. "The History of Critical Music." *Dominant*, 1 (April 1928), supplement, iv-v.

8. "John Masefield." *Saturday Review of Literature*, 6 (June 28, 1930), 1152-55.

9. "Introduction to the Second Edition." *Poems of Gerard Manley Hopkins*. Ed. Robert Bridges. London: Oxford University Press, 1930, rpt. 1931, 1933, 1935, in the Oxford Bookshelf 1937, 1938. Pp. ix-xvi.

10. "Gerard Manley Hopkins." *Times Literary Supplement,*
    1 January 1931, p. 12.

    A letter.

11. "T. S. Eliot." *Selected Modern English Essays.*
    Second Series. World's Classics Series. London:
    Oxford University Press, 1932, rpt. 1935,
    1938, 1942, 1945, 1949, 1956, 1962. Pp. 278-87.

12. "Autocriticism." *The Week-End Review,* 8
    (November 18, 1933), 525.

    Williams comments upon his *Reason and Beauty in the Poetic
    Mind* (I-A-iv-3).

13. "Lord Macaulay." *Six Short Biographies.* Ed.
    R. C. and N. Goffin. Indian Branch of Oxford
    University Press, 1933. Pp. 85-100.

    Reprinted in *Image* (I-A-iv-6), pp. 6-14.

14. "Robert Bridges." *English Critical Essays, Twentieth
    Century.* Ed. Phyllis M. Jones. London: Oxford
    University Press, 1933. Pp. 290-301.

    First published in *Poetry at Present,* 1930 (I-A-iv-1).

15. "Landor." *Imaginary Conversations* by Walter
    Savage Landor. Ed. F. A. Cavanaugh and A. C. Ward.
    London: Oxford University Press, 1934. Pp. v-xi.

    Reprinted in *Image* (I-A-iv-6), pp. 15-19.

16. "Introduction." *The New Book of English Verse.*
    Ed. Charles Williams. London: V. Gollancz,
    1935; New York: Macmillan, 1936. Pp. 3-18.

17. "Henry V." *Shakespeare Criticism, 1919-35.* Selected
    with an introduction by Anne Bradby. World's
    Classics Series. London: Oxford University
    Press, 1936, rpt. 1937, 1941, 1945, 1949.
    Pp. 180-88.

18. "Troilus and Cressida" and "Hamlet." *Shakespeare Criticism, 1919-35*. Selected with an introduction by Anne Bradby. World's Classics Series. London: Oxford University Press, 1936, rpt. 1937, 1941, 1945, 1949. Pp. 188-208.

19. "A Poet's Papers." *Time and Tide*, 18 (February 20, 1937), 238.

    A letter.

20. "Notes on Religious Drama." *Chelmsford Diocesan Chronicle*, 23 (May 1937), 75-76.

21. "The New Milton." *St. Martin's Review*, 36 (July 1937), 255-61.

    Two alterations in the views of Milton, one concerning his biography and the other, the reading of his verse, encourage a fresh approach to interpretation. Reprinted in *Image* (I-A-iv-6), pp. 19-25.

22. "Byron and Byronism." *Bulletin* of the British Institute of the University of Paris (April 1938), pp. 13-19.

    Lecture.

23. "Religious Drama." *Good Speech* (Quarterly Review of the Speech Fellowship, April 1938).

    Reprinted in *Image* (I-A-iv-6), pp. 55-59.

24. "Antichrist and the City's Laws." *Time and Tide*, 19 (August 27, 1938), 1195-97.

    Williams defines the Antichrist as one who refuses to be the "foolish and joyous equal of men and women." Reprinted in *Image* (I-A-iv-6), pp. 117-21.

25. "Sound and Variations." *Time and Tide*, 19 (September 3, 1938), 1218-20.

    Williams points out the lack of emphasis upon sound in human experience. Reprinted in *Image* (I-A-iv-6), pp. 51-55.

26. "Queen Victoria." *More Short Biographies*. Ed.
    R. C. Goffin. London: Oxford University
    Press, 1938. Pp. 29-49.

27. "H. M. P." *Lantern* (Oxford University Press
    Publication, January 1939), pp. 98-101.

    Unsigned article on Helen M. Peacock.

28. "Sensuality and Substance." *Theology*, 38 (May
    1939), 352-60.

    Williams discusses Dante's romantic experience and
    the Affirmation of Images as ways to attain unity of body and
    soul in the approach to God. The secondary subject
    is D. H. Lawrence, who recognized the importance
    of the body and sex but failed to see certain implications.
    Reprinted in *Image* (I-A-iv-6), pp. 68-75.

29. "Gerard Hopkins and Milton." *Poetry Review*, 30
    (July/August 1939), 307-08.

    A letter.

30. "The Church Looks Forward." *St. Martin's Review*, No.
    593 (July 1940), 329-32.

    Williams believes the Way of Affirmation of Images must
    become a central concern of the Church. Reprinted
    in *Image* (I-A-iv-6), pp. 154-58.

31. "The Image of the City in English Verse." *Dublin
    Review*, 207 (July 1940), 39-51.

    Williams defines the image of the City as "the sense of many
    relationships between men and women woven into a
    unity." He explores the use of this image in the works of
    Wordsworth, Shakespeare, Milton and Eliot. Reprinted
    in *Image* (I-A-iv-6), pp. 92-102.

32. "Taste in Literature." *Listener*, 24 (December 26,
    1940), 913-14.

    A discussion with E. Sydney and D. Hawkins.

33. "The Recovery of Spiritual Initiative." *Christendom* (A Journal of Christian Sociology), 10 (December 1940), 238-49.

34. "Introduction." *The English Poems of John Milton.* World's Classics Series. London: Oxford University Press, 1940, rpt. 1951. Pp. vii-xx.

    Reprinted in *Image* (I-A-iv-6), pp. 26-36.

35. "Introduction." *The Present Age* by Sören Kierkegaard. Trans. Alexander Dru and Walter Lowrie. London: Oxford University Press, 1940. Pp. vii-xii.

36. "Notes on the Way." *Time and Tide,* 22 (February 28, 1941), 170-71.

    Williams discusses his myth, particularly the use of the female body as a symbol of the ancient Roman Empire and the meaning of Logres.

37. "Notes on the Way." *Time and Tide,* 22 (March 7, 1941), 194-95.

38. "Charles Williams on *Taliessin through Logres.*" *Poetry Review,* 32 (March/April 1941), 77-81.

    Williams explains that *Taliessin* began with his disappointment in Tennyson's treatment of the Grail as a subject. Certain technical details and concepts connected with Williams's cycle of poems are discussed. Reprinted in *Image* (I-A-iv-6), as the "Making of Taliessin," pp. 179-83.

39. "Blake and Wordsworth." *Dublin Review,* 208 (April 1941), 175-86.

    The *Prophetic Books* and the *Prelude,* similar in that they deal with the fall and redemption of England, approached through this similarity. Reprinted in *Image* (I-A-iv-6), pp. 59-67.

40. "The War for Compassion." *Sword of the Spirit,* No. 20 (May 15, 1941), p. 7.

41. "Deportment in Criticism." *Poetry Review*, 32 (May/June 1941), 188.

    A letter.

42. "Notes on the Way." *Time and Tide*, 22 (September 13, 1941), 769.

    The subject is the war.

43. "Charles Williams's 'Notes on the Way,' " *Time and Tide*, 22 (September 27, 1941), 818.

    A letter.

44. "Paracelsus." *Time and Tide*, 22 (September 27, 1941), 820-21.

45. "The Redeemed City." *Dublin Review*, 209 (October 1941), 120-28.

    The central idea is that for Christians there is no final idea "but the glory of God in the redeemed and universal union—call it Man or the Church or the City." Reprinted in *Image* (I-A-iv-6), pp. 102-10.

46. "Natural Goodness." *Theology*, 43 (October 1941), 211-16.

    Williams's ideas about the Incarnation, the Fall of man, and the Redemption. Reprinted in *Image* (I-A-iv-6), pp. 75-80.

47. "Religion and Love in Dante: The Theology of Romantic Love." Dacre Papers, No. 6. Westminister: Dacre Press, 1941. 40 pp.

    A brief exploration. An expanded treatment of "romantic love" is to be found in *Figure of Beatrice* (I-A-iv-4).

48. "The Way of Exchange." New Foundation Papers, No. 2. London: James Clarke, 1941. p. 23.

    Williams asserts that the idea of exchange is the basis of the Christian and natural life. Reprinted in *Image* (I-A-iv-6), pp. 147-54.

49. "Notes on the Way." *Time and Tide*, 23 (February 28, 1942), 170-71.

50. "Notes on the Way." *Time and Tide*, 23 (March 7, 1942), 194-95.

51. "Easter Letter." *Poetry Magazine*, St. John's, London (April 1942).

52. "St. John of the Cross." *Time and Tide*, 23 (June 27, 1942), 522.

53. "The Index of the Body." *Dublin Review*, 211 (July 1942), 13-20.

    Through the body we experience the Kingdom of God, by neglecting it we neglect the Kingdom itself. Reprinted in *Image* (I-A-iv-6), pp. 80-87.

54. "A Dialogue on Mr. Eliot's Poem." *Dublin Review*, 212 (April 1943), 114-22.

55. "Hell." *St. Albans Diocesan Magazine*, England (April 1943).

56. "A Dialogue on Hierarchy." *Time and Tide*, 24 (October 2, 1943), 799.

    The dialogue suggests that a changing hierarchy appears in all things but equality is the sum of all the changes. Reprinted in *Image* (I-A-iv-6), pp. 127-30.

57. "Personalism?" *Time and Tide*, 24 (November 27, 1943), 971.

    The letter to the editor concerns a review.

58. "Introduction." *The Letters of Evelyn Underhill*. London: Longmans, Green, 1943, rpt. 1944, 1956. Pp. 7-46.

59. "What the Cross Means to Me." *What the Cross Means to Me: A Theological Symposium*. London: James Clarke, 1943. Pp. 168-77.

    The essay concerns the symbolism of the cross in relation to substitution and exchange. Reprinted in *Image* (I-A-iv-6), pp. 131-39.

60. "The Jews and Jacques Maritain." *Time and Tide*, 25 (January 8, 1944), 25.

    A letter.

61. "Tasso." *Time and Tide*, 25 (March 11, 1944), 216.

62. "Malory and the Grail Legend." *Dublin Review*, 214 (April 1944), 144-53.

    In Williams's mind, Malory does not fully explore the potential of the Grail story. Williams suggests the possibilities he sees for Galahad and other of the mythical elements. Reprinted in *Image* (I-A-iv-6), pp. 186-94.

63. "On the Poetry of The Duchess of Malfi." *The Duchess of Malfi* by John Webster. London: Sylvan Press, 1945. Pp. xv-xxii.

D. Reviews

1. *Folly and Other Poems*: Theodore Maynard. *New Witness*, 12 (August 2, 1918), 277.

2. *Carven from the Laurel Tree, Essays*: Theodore Maynard. *New Witness*, 13 (March 28, 1919), 444.

3. *William Blake, The Man*: Charles Gardner. *New Witness*, 15 (December 5, 1919), 50-51.

4. *Essays in Art*: A. Clutton-Brock. *New Witness*, 15 (March 12, 1920), 313-14.

5. *Poems*: Everilda Parker; *Ambush and Song*: M. G. Field; *A Student's Love Songs*: T. H. Collinson; *Playing Poet in the South*: E. W. .Thomas; *Primal Airs*: J. A. M. Alcock; *The Gate of Bronze*: T. W. Earp; *Dryad's Trove and Other Poems*: Elizabeth Mott. *New Witness*, 15 (March 19, 1920), 334-35.

6. *An Anthology of Catholic Poets*: Shane Leslie, comp.; *The Wedding Sermon*: Coventry Patmore. *G. K.'s Weekly*, 2 (January 30, 1926), 494.

7. *The Cobra Candlestick*: E. Barker; *Peril at Cranbury Hall*: John Rhode; *The Mystery of Vincent Dane*: Mrs. Victor Rickard; *The Secret of the Sapphire Ring*: M. V. Woodgate. *Daily News and Westminster Gazette* (January 24, 1930), p. 4.

8. *Dynamite Drury Again*: L. Patrick Greeses; *A Brideport Dagger*: John Milbrook; *It Walks by Night*: John Dickson Carr; *Death in the Dark*: Stacey Bishop. *Daily News and Westminster Gazette* (April 10, 1930), p. 4.

9. *Mr. Fortune Explains*: H. C. Bailey; *The Best Detective
   Stories of the Year 1929*; *The Fifth Victim*: Dale
   Collins; *Suspect*: Gerard Fairlie. *Daily News
   and Westminster Gazette* (April 17, 1930), p. 4.

10. *The Bowery Murder*: Willard K. Smith; *Shock*:
    Virgil Markham; *The Noose*: Philip MacDonald.
    Daily News and Westminster Gazette (May 8, 1930),
    p. 4.

11. *The Two Ticket Puzzles*: J. J. Connington; *The
    King Against Anne Bickerton*: Sydney Fowler;
    The Secret of the Cove: H. L. Deakin. *Daily News and
    Westminster Gazette* (May 27, 1930), p. 4.

12. *Burglars in Bucks*: G. D. H. and M. Cole;
    The Hardway Diamonds Mystery: Miles Burton;
    The Lady of Despair: Francis D. Grierson; *Post
    Mortem*: Gilbert Collins; *A Clue in Wax*: Fred
    M. White. *Daily News and Chronicle* (June 4, 1930),
    p.4.

13. *The Komani Mystery*: Victor Sampson; *The Green
    Complex*: Harold MacGrath; *The Night Club
    Mystery*: Elizabeth Jordon; *Murder from Beyond*:
    R. Francis Foster; *The League of Discontent*:
    Francis Beeding. *Daily News and Chronicle*
    (June 11, 1930), p. 4.

14. *The Person Called Z*: Jefferson Farjeon; *The Subtle
    Trail*: Joseph Gollomb; *The Shop Window
    Murders*: Vernon Loder; *Murder on the Palisades*:
    Will Levinrew; *The House in Tuesday Market*:
    J. S. Fletcher; *Slane's Long Shots*: E. Phillips
    Oppenheim. *News Chronicle* (July 7, 1930), p. 4.

15. *Rudi Schneider, A Scientific Study of his Mediumship*:
    Harry Price. *News Chronicle* (July 24, 1930)
    p. 4.

16. *Q.E.D.*: Lyn Brock; *Pinehurst*: John Rhode; *The Owner Lies Dead*: Tyline Perry; *The Crystal Beads Murder*: Annie Haynes. *News Chronicle* (July 30, 1930), p. 4.

17. *The Mark of the Rat*: Arnold Fredericks; *The Avenging Ikon*: Charles Barry; *The Man with the Squeaky Voice*: R. A. J. Walling; *The Bainbridge Murder*: Cortland Fitzsimmons. *News Chronicle* (August 6, 1930), p. 4.

18. *The Cauldron Bubbles*: N. A. Temple-Ellis; *The Obole of Paradise*: Agnes Miller; *Dead Man Twice*: Christopher Bush; *Camouflage*: Lawrence W. Meynell. *News Chronicle* (August 14, 1930), p. 4.

19. *The Dying Alderman*: Henry Wade; *The Body on the Bus*: Leonard Hollingworth; *The Gold and Copper Delamonds*: Agnes Autumn; *The Terror of the Torlands*: T. C. H. Jacobs. *News Chronicle* (August 26, 1930), p. 4.

20. *Death in a Deckchair*: Milward Kennedy; *Seven Suspects*: Florence Ryerson and Colin Clements; *When No Man Pursueth*: David Sharp; *Diamonds of Death*: Hilda Willett. *News Chronicle* (September 3, 1930), p. 4.

21. *The Museum Murder*: John T. McIntyre; *I Like a Good Murder*: Marcus Magill; *The Brazen Confession*: Cecil Freeman Gregg. *News Chronicle* (September 9, 1930), p. 4.

22. *Sir John Magill's Last Journey*: Freeman Wills Crofts; *The Body on the Floor*: Nancy Barr Mavity; *The Folded Paper Mystery*: Hulbert Footner. *News Chronicle* (September 15, 1930), p. 4.

23. *Saint Augustine*: Giovanni Papini. *News Chronicle*
    (September 18, 1930), p. 4.

24. *Strong Poison*: Dorothy L. Sayers; *The Murder of
    Cecily Thane*: H. Ashbrook; *The Murder
    House*: T. Arthur Plummer, *News Chronicle*
    (September 18, 1930), p. 4.

25. *Mr. Pottermack's Oversight*: R. Austin Freeman;
    The Peering One: Evander Murray; *The
    Murder at the Vicarage*: Agatha Christie. *News
    Chronicle* (October 14, 1930), p. 4.

26. *Heinrich Heine, A Critical Examination*: H. Walter;
    W. E. Henley, A Memoir: Kennedy Williamson; *George
    Eliot, A Study*: J. Lewis May; *Her South African
    Ancestors*: S. C. Cronwright. *News Chronicle*
    (October 16, 1930), p. 4.

27. *Dr. Krastnki's Secret*: M. P. Shiel; *The French
    Powder Mystery*: Ellery Queen; *The Death of Dr.
    Whitelaw*: A. Wilson. *News Chronicle* (October 21,
    1930), p. 4.

28. *Plain Murder*: C. S. Forester; *Mystery on the Moor*:
    J. Jefferson Farjeon; *Corpse in Canonicals*:
    G. D. H. and M. Cole. *News Chronicle* (November 4,
    1930), p. 4.

29. *Crime at Keeper's*: Thomas Cobb; *The Hymn Tune
    Mystery*: George Birmingham; *Murder Backstairs*: Anne
    Austin. *News Chronicle* (November 6, 1930),
    p. 4.

30. *Eight Victorian Poets*: F. L. Lucas. *News Chronicle*
    (November 25, 1930), p. 4.

31. *Horror Comes to Thripplands*: Gilbert Collins;
    Murder at the Pageant: Victor L. Whitechurch;

The Mysterious Mademoiselle: Francis D. Grierson. News Chronicle (December 1, 1930), p. 4.

32. Heaven: Frank Townsend; Poems New and Old: R. H. Mottram; Dear Judas: Robinson Jeffers; Deserted House: Dorothy Wellesley; A Broadcast Anthology of Modern Poetry: Dorothy Wellesley, ed. News Chronicle (December 9, 1930), p. 4.

33. The Tragedy of the Chinese Mine: Ian Greig; The Ticker-Tape Murder: Milton M. Propper; Crowner's Quest: Adam Broome. News Chronicle (December 24, 1930), p. 4.

34. The Poems of Lascelles Abercrombie. News Chronicle (December 29, 1930), p. 4.

35. The Strangler Fig: John Stephen Strange; The Other Bullet: Nancy Barr Mavity; Tragedy on the Line: John Rhode. News Chronicle (January 5, 1931), p. 4.

36. Who Cut the Colonel's Throat?: Laing Hay; The Box Hill Murder: J. S. Fletcher; Murder in the Mirror: W. W. Masters. News Chronicle (January 21, 1931), p. 4.

37. The Bell Street Murders: Sydney Fowler; The Moment After: Virginia Tracey; The Tragedy of Draythorpe: Leo Grex. News Chronicle (February 9, 1931), p. 4.

38. Inspector Bedison and the Sunderland Case: Thomas Cobb; Proof Counter Proof: E. R. Punshon; Murder by Latitude: Rufus King. News Chronicle (February 18, 1931), p. 4.

39. *Quest*: N. Temple-Ellis; *The Great Southern Mystery*:
G. D. H. and M. Cole; *The Three Crimes*: Miles
Burton; *The Murder of Geraldine Foster*: Anthony
Abbot. *News Chronicle* (March 2, 1931), p. 4.

40. *The Sale of St. Thomas*: Lascelles Abercrombie.
News Chronicle (March 5, 1931), p. 4.

41. *Dr. Watson*: S. C. Roberts. *News Chronicle* (March 9,
1931), p. 4.

42. *Malice Aforethought*: Francis Hes; *Tell No
Tales*: George Limnelius; *Found Drowned*: Eden
Philpotts. *News Chronicle* (March 18, 1931), p. 4.

43. *The Avenging Parrot*: Anne Austin; *Mystery in the
Channel*: F. Wills Crofts; *The Choice*: Philip
MacDonald; *A Murder of Some Importance*: Bruce
Graeme. *News Chronicle* (April 6, 1931), p. 5.

44. *Murder in Earl's Court*: Neil Gordon; *Murder out of
Tune*: Marcus Magill; *The Four Answers*: John
Cobnor. *News Chronicle* (April 7, 1931), p. 4.

45. *The Fleet Hall Inheritance*: Richard Keverne;
The House with No Address: E. M. Channon;
My Particular Murder: David Sharp; *The Horror
of the Juvenal Manse*: Kenneth Perkins. *News
Chronicle* (April 15, 1931), p. 4.

46. *Killing No Murder*: M. G. Kiddy; *The Jungle
Crime*: Luke Allen; *The Mystery of Hunting's End*:
M. G. Eberhart; *Whereabouts Unknown*: Mrs.
Baillie Reynolds. *News Chronicle* (May 5, 1931), p. 4.

47. *Corpse in Cold Storage*: Milward Kennedy;
Author in Distress: C. M. Mills; *Danger in the Dark*:
A. K. Chase; *Encore the Lone Wolf*: Louis
Joseph Vance. *News Chronicle* (May 11, 1931), p. 6.

48. *Crime in the Arcade*: Walter Proudfoot; *Cat and Feather*: Don Basil; *The Monkshood Murder*: A. C. and Carmen Eddington. *News Chronicle* (May 19, 1931), p. 4.

49. *The Upfold Farm Mystery*: A. Fielding; *The Hanging Woman*: John Rhode; *The Great London Mystery*: Charles Kingston. *News Chronicle* (June 10, 1931), p. 4.

50. *Three Yards of Cord*: Collin Brooks; *Dancing Death*: Christopher Bush; *And Then Silence*: Milton M. Propper. *News Chronicle* (June 17, 1931), p. 4.

51. *Live Wire*: Austen Allen; *The Night of Fear*: Moray Dalton; *Murder at Monk's Farm*: Cecil Waye. *News Chronicle* (July 15, 1931), p. 4.

52. *The Crime Without a Flaw*: Leslie Despard; *The Sands of Windee*: Arthur W. Upfield; *The Stolen Cellini*: Alan Thomas. *News Chronicle* (July 30, 1931), p. 4.

53. *Blood Money*: John Goodwin; *The Swan Island Mystery*: Victoria Lincoln; *Jaws of Circumstance*: Carl Clausen. *News Chronicle* (August 25, 1931), p. 4.

54. *The Sittaford Mystery*: Agatha Christie; *The Wraith*: Philip MacDonald; *Hue and Cry*: Bruce Hamilton. *News Chronicle* (September 7, 1931), p. 4.

55. *The Winning Trick*: Neville Brand; *The Hanging of Constance Hillier*: Sydney Fowler; *The Hangman's Guests*: Stuart Martin; *The Riddle of the Winged Death*: Hazel Phillips Hanshew. *News Chronicle* (September 16, 1931), p. 4.

56. *The Crime in the Dutch Garden*: Herbert Adams; *Mystery at Friar's Pardon*: Martin Porlock; *The Crime of Century*: Anthony Abbot. *News Chronicle* (October 7, 1931), p. 4.

57. *The Rembrandt Murder*: Henry James Forman;
    The Secret of the Swamp: George Bettany; *The Double
    Solution*: Cecil Freeman Gregg; *Murder! Murder!*:
    Lawrence Vail. *News Chronicle* (October 22,
    1931), p. 4.

58. *Harbour*: Philip MacDonald; *Unsolved*: Bruce
    Graeme; *Red Stain*: Vernon Loder; *Murder in
    the Fine Degree*: J. S. Fletcher. *News Chronicle*
    (November 17, 1931), p. 4.

59. *Dead Man's Watch*: G. D. H. and M. Cole;
    Murder Game: Stephen Strange; *Murder at
    Lintercombe*: Ian Greig; *Death Rides the Forest*:
    Rupert Grayson. *News Chronicle* (December
    9, 1931), p. 4.

60. *Common Sense about Poetry*: L. A. G. Strong;
    Selected Poems: L. A. G. Strong; *Parody and
    Dust Shot*: G. F. Bradby; *Fatal Interview*: Edna St.
    Vincent Millay; *East London Poems*: A. K. Sabin.
    News Chronicle (December 14, 1931), p. 4.

61. *Murder at School*: Glen Trevor; *Stop Press*: Erle
    Spencer. *News Chronicle* (January 1, 1932),
    p. 4.

62. *The Body on the Beam*: Anthony Gilbert; *Sudden Death*:
    Freeman Wills Crofts; *Dead Man's Music*:
    Christopher Bush. *News Chronicle* (January 7,
    1932), p. 4.

63. *New English Poems, A Miscellany of Contemporary
    Verse*: Lascelles Abercrombie. *News Chronicle*
    (January 13, 1932), p. 4.

64. *Climax at the Falls*: Gregory Baxter; *The Polo Ground
    Mystery*: Robin Forsythe; *Murder in the Squire's
    Pew*: J. S. Fletcher. *News Chronicle* (January
    25, 1932), p. 4.

65. *Genius in Murder*: E. R. Punshon; *Cut Throat*:
Christopher Bush; *The Devil Drives*: Virgil Markham;
Turmoil at Brede: Seldon Truss. *News Chronicle*
(February 10, 1932), p. 4.

66. *Mystery in Kensington Gore*: Martin Porlock;
Murder of the Night Club Lady: Anthony Abbot;
Mad-Doctor Merciful: Collin Brooks; *Moran
Chambers Smiled*: E. Phillips Oppenheim. *News
Chronicle* (March 7, 1932), p. 4.

67. *Fourth Degree*: K. S. Daiger; *I Stood in the Shadow of
the Black Cap*: Jackson Budd; *The Bancaster
Mystery*: A. N. Hodges. *News Chronicle* (March 16,
1932), p. 4.

68. *Murder in the Dentist's Chair*: Mally Thynne;
The Death Film: P. R. Shore; *Death Must Have
Laughed*: John F. Turner; *The Bird Cage*: Eimar
O'Duffy. *News Chronicle* (March 22, 1932),
p. 4.

69. *Murder in the Zoo*: Babette Hughes; *Bullets
Bite Deep*: David Hume; *The End of Mr. Davidson*:
Oliver Stoner. *News Chronicle* (April 27,
1932), p. 4.

70. *Murder in the Basement*: Anthony Berkeley; *Gigins
Court*: Bruce Graeme; *Which of Them?*: Peter
Black. *News Chronicle* (June 2, 1932), p. 4.

71. *The Division Bell Mystery*: Ellen Wilkinson; *The
Theatre Crime*: Fred Andrews; *Murder at the
Moorings*: Miles Burton; *The Casual Murderer*: Hulbert
Footner. *News Chronicle* (July 5, 1932), p. 4.

72. *Tiger Standish*: Sydney Horler; *The Mystery of
the Monkey-Gland Cocktail*: Roger East; *The Cast to
Death*: Nigel Orde-Powlett; *Chinese Red*: Gilbert
Collins. *News Chronicle* (July 18, 1932), p. 4.

73. *The Greek Coffin Mystery*: Ellery Queen; *I, the Criminal*: David Sharp; *Murder in the Cellar*: Louise Eppley and Rebecca Gayton. *News Chronicle* (July 28, 1932), p. 4.

74. *Spectral Evidence*: Robert Hare; *Murder Could Not Kill*: Gregory Baxter; *Six Lines*: N. A. Temple-Ellis. *News Chronicle* (August 23, 1932), p. 4.

75. *The New Morality*: G. E. Newsom. *News Chronicle* (September 7, 1932), p. 4.

76. *Plot Against a Widow*: R. C. Ashby; *The Public School Murder*: W. C. Woodthorpe; *The Gilt-Edged Mystery*: E. M. Channon. *News Chronicle* (September 21, 1932), p. 4.

77. *Rope to Spare*: Philip MacDonald; *Lobelia Grove*: Anthony Rolls; *Cottage Sinister*: O. Patrick; *The Eternal Moment*: G. B. H. Logan. *News Chronicle* (October 7, 1932), p. 4.

78. *Murder at the College*: Victor L. Whitechurch; *The By-Pass Murder*: David Frome; *Trunk Call*: J. Jefferson Farjeon; *A Hundred Mysteries for Armchair Detectives*: J. C. Connell. *News Chronicle* (December 13, 1932), p. 4.

79. *Murder by Formula*: J. H. Wallis; *When Rogues Fall Out*: R. Austin Freeman; *Death of a Star*: G. D. H. and M. Cole; *Ben Sees It Through*: J. Jefferson Farjeon. *News Chronicle* (December 21, 1932), p. 4.

80. *Poison in Jest*: J. D. Carr; *The Secret of the Dark Room*: Robert J. Casey; *The Body Behind the Bar*: C. F. Gregg; *The Water Witch*: Russell Thorndyke. *News Chronicle* (January 3, 1933), p. 4.

81. *The Murder of Caroline Bundy*: Alice Campbell; *Death on My Left*: Philip MacDonald; *The Thousandth Case*: George Dilnot; *The Channel Million*:

Gilbert Collins. *News Chronicle* (January 31, 1933), p. 4.

82. *The Wailing Rock Murders*: Clifford Orr; *Murders of an Initiate*: Milton M. Propper; *Dead Man's Alibi*: Leonard Hollingworth; *Who Killed Alfred Snowe?*: J. S. Fletcher. *News Chronicle* (February 13, 1933), p. 4.

83. *The Ebony Mirror*: F. A. Gallimore; *The Corpse on the White House Lawn*: "Diplomat"; *Why Shoot a Butler?*: Georgette Heyer. *News Chronicle* (March 1, 1933), p. 4.

84. *The Hog's Back Mystery*: F. W. Crofts; *The Two Undertakers*: Francis Beeding; *Death in the Forest*: Neville Brand; *Under London*: Val Gielgud and Holt Marvell. *News Chronicle* (April 7, 1933), p. 4.

85. *R.I.P.*: Philip MacDonald; *The Kennel Murder Case*: S. S. Van Dine; *The Man Who Shook the Earth*: Sydney Horler; *Slade Scores Again*: Richard Essex. *News Chronicle* (April 26, 1933), p. 4.

86. *Erasmus*: Christopher Hollis. *Time and Tide*, 14 (April 29, 1933), 517-18.

87. *An Oxford Tragedy*: J. C. Masterman; *There Sits Death*: Paul McGuire; *Traitor's Rock*: G. E. Rochester; *Murder at Pringlehurst*: James Corbett. *News Chronicle* (June 5, 1933), p. 5.

88. *The American Gun Mystery*: Ellery Queen; *The Claverton Mystery*: John Rhode; *Harlequin of Death*: Sydney Horler; *Gun Justice*: Jackson Cole; *Many Mysteries*: E. P. Oppenheim. *News Chronicle* (June 14, 1933), p. 7.

89. *The Fate of Jane McKenzie*: N. B. Mavity; *Death Comes at Night*: Kenneth Ingram; *Dover-Ostend*: Taffrail; *Dr. Greenfingers*: Edward Woodward. *News Chronicle* (July 26, 1933), p. 7.

90. *The Tragedy of Tolstoy*: Countess Alexandra Tolstoy. *Listener*, 10 (August 9, 1933), 218.

91. *Trial by Virgins*: David Larg. *Week-End Review*, 8 (August 12, 1933), 168-69.

92. *Poems*: Edward Shanks. *Week-End Review*, 8 (August 26, 1933), 213-14.

93. *The English Galaxy, An Anthology of Shorter Poems*: Gerald Bullett, ed. *Week-End Review*, 8 (September 9, 1933), 275.

94. *The Second Case of Mr. Paul Savoy*: Jackson Gregory; *The Bank Vault Mystery*: Louis F. Booth; *The Lonely Inn Mystery*: Leo Grex; *The Amateur Murderer*: Carroll J. Daly; *The Menace*: Sydney Horler. *News Chronicle* (September 8, 1933), p. 7.

95. *A Popular History of English Poetry*: T. Earle Welby. *Week-End Review*, 8 (October 7, 1933), supplement 358-59.

96. *Murder Is Easy*: Armstrong Livingston; *Death on the Oxford Road*: E. C. R. Lorac; *The Affair at Aliquid*: G. D. H. and M. I. Cole; *Other Man's Danger*: Maxwell March; *The Case of the Velvet Claws*: E. S. Gardner. *News Chronicle* (October 27, 1933), p. 4.

97. *Reason and Beauty in the Poetic Mind*: Charles Williams. *Week-End Review*, 8 (November 18, 1933), 525.

98. *Redhead*: John Creasey; *The Double Smile*: Maurice
LeBlanc; *Death Comes to Fanshawe*: James
Corbett; *The Wrong Murder Mystery*: Charles Barry;
Fatality in Fleet Street: C. St. John Sprigg. *News
Chronicle* (December 22, 1933), p. 4.

99. *Mr. Fortune Wonders*: H. C. Bailey; *The Bride of
Fu-Manchu*: Sax Rohmer; *The Clue of the Dead
Goldfish*: Victor McClure; *The Secret of
Tangles*: L. R. Gribble; *The Judson Murder Case*:
E. A. Aldrich. *News Chronicle* (December 29, 1933),
p. 4.

100. *The Nine Tailors*: Dorothy L. Sayers; *The
Dragon Murder Case*: S. S. Van Dine; *Murder on the
Orient Express*: Agatha Christie; *A Dagger in Fleet
Street*: R. C. Woodthorpe; *By Misadventure*: Alan
Brock. *News Chronicle* (January 17, 1934), p. 4.

101. *The Gallows of Chance*: E. Phillips Oppenheim;
Marriage and Murder: David Sharp; *The Orange
Ray*: Maurice G. Kiddy; *Murder at Grasmere Abbey*:
Maurice B. Dix; *The Campden Ruby Murder*:
Adam Bliss. *News Chronicle* (February 2, 1934), p. 4.

102. *Gallows Alley*: Anthony Skene; *The Mysterious
Mr. Badman*: W. F. Harvey; *Murder in Trinidad*: John W.
Vandercook; *The Red Flame of Erinpura*: Talbot
Mundy; *They Came by Night*: Seldon Truss. *News
Chronicle* (February 20, 1934), p. 4.

103. *12:30 from Croydon*: Freeman Wills Crofts;
Obelisks en Route: C. Daly King; *Death at
Broadcasting House*: Val Gielgud and Holt Marvell;
The Murder of a Midget: M. J. Freeman. *News
Chronicle* (March 15, 1934), p. 4.

104. *End and Beginning*: John Masefield; *Spoils of Time*: Willoughby Weaving; *Elegies and Songs*: John Mavrogordato; *John Lord, Satirist*: George R. Hamilton; *The Tragedy of Man*: Imre Madach. *Time and Tide*, 15 (April 21, 1934), 510, 512.

105. *Murder at the Eclipse*: John Alexander; *Murder— Nine and Out*: J. V. Turner; *Murder to Measure*: Robert Mason; *Fool's Gold*: S. H. Page; *Smash and Grab*: Clifton Robbins. *News Chronicle* (May 1, 1934), p. 4.

106. *Still Dead*: Ronald A. Knox; *Death in the Quarry*: G. D. H. and M. Cole; *The Portcullis Room*: Valentine Williams; *Stark Naked*: Lawrence R. Bourne. *News Chronicle* (June 4, 1934), p. 4.

107. *The Cross-Word Mystery*: E. R. Punshon; *The Thin Man*: Dashiel Hammett; *Plan XVI*: Douglas G. Browne; *The 3-7-9 Murder*: Grey Morton. *News Chronicle* (June 18, 1934), p. 4.

108. *Constable, Guard Thyself*: Henry Wade; *Murder on the Cliff*: Clive Ryland; *The Bell is Answered*: Roger East; *An International Affair*: Bruce Graeme; *Death by the Mistletoe*: Angus MacVicar. *News Chronicle* (August 3, 1934), p. 4.

109. *As They Rise*: E. Laurie Long; *Ten Hours*: Harry S. Keeler; *The Diamond Ransom Murders*: Nellie Child; *The Five Suspects*: R. A. J. Walling. *News Chronicle* (January 23, 1935), p. 4.

110. *Three Act Tragedy*: Agatha Christie; *Death in a Little Town*: R. C. Woodthorpe; *The Ragged Robin Murders*: Guy Morton; *Frame Up*: Collin Brooks; *The Crooked Sign*: Ben Bolt; *Dames Errant*:

George Norsworthy. *News Chronicle* (February 15, 1935), p. 4.

111. *Victoria of England*: Edith Sitwell. *G. K.'s Weekly*, 22 (March 5, 1936), 382-83.

112. *The Home University Library. G. K.'s Weekly*, 23 (April 2, 1936), 52-53.

113. "The Biography of Mr. William Hayley": William Hayley. *G. K.'s Weekly*, 23 (April 30, 1936), 114-15.

114. *Trent's Own Case*: E. C. Bentley and H. Warner Allen. *G. K.'s Weekly*, 23 (May 28, 1936), 178-79.

115. *An Essay on the Restoration of Property*: Hilaire Belloc. *G. K.'s Weekly*, 23 (June 18, 1936), 229-30.

116. *Murder off Miami*: Dennis Wheatley and J. G. Hinks. *G. K.'s Weekly*, 23 (July 23, 1936), 306-07.

117. *Henry Crabb Robinson*: J. M. Baker. *Sunday Times* (London) (March 7, 1937), p. 15.

118. *The Laughing Prophet*: Emile Cammaerts. *Sunday Times* (May 30, 1937), p. 14.

119. *The Riddle of Napoleon*: Raoul Brice; *Bonaparte*: Eugene Tarle, John Cournos, trans. *Sunday Times* (June 6, 1937), p. 12.

120. *Drama and Society in the Age of Jonson*: L. C. Knights; *Shakespeare Biography and Other Papers*: Felix E. Schelling. *Sunday Times* (July 4, 1937), p. 8.

121. *Saul of Tarsus*: F. Warburton Lewis; *St. Augustine of Hippo*: Hugh Pope. *Sunday Times* (September 12, 1937), p. 7.

122. *Why Was Lincoln Murdered?*: Otto Eisenschiml.
Sunday Times (September 26, 1937), p. 10.

123. *Father Brown on Chesterton*: John O'Connor.
Sunday Times (October 10, 1937), p. 8.

124. *Shakespeare's Plays, A Commentary*: M. R. Ridley.
Sunday Times (October 17, 1937), p. 13.

125. *Trial of Lizzie Borden*: Edmund Pearson, ed. *Sunday Times* (November 14, 1937), p. 15.

126. *A Vision*: W. B. Yeats. *Time and Tide*, 18
(December 4, 1937), 1674-76.

127. *Mightier Than the Sword*: Ford Maddox Ford.
Time and Tide, 19 (March 12, 1938), 350.

128. *The Kingdom of God and the Son of Man*: Rudolph
Otto. *London Mercury*, 37 (March 1938), 553.

129. *Rainer Marie Rilke, Aspects of His Mind and Poetry*:
William Rose and G. Craig Houston, eds. *Time and Tide*, 19 (April 9, 1938), 500-02.

130. *Wallenstein, Soldier Under Saturn*: Francis Watson.
Sunday Times (May 8, 1938), p. 12.

131. *General Washington's Dilemma*: Katherine
Mayo. *Sunday Times* (May 15, 1938), p. 7.

132. *Wesley's England*: J. H. Whiteley; *England, Before and After Wesley*: J. Wesley Bready. *Time and Tide*,
19 (May 21, 1938), 722-23.

133. *The Miltonic Setting*: E. M. W. Tillyard. *London Mercury*, 38 (May 1938), 82.

134. *Arthur Rimbaud*: Enid Starkie. *Time and Tide*, 19
(June 11, 1938), 832.

135. *Studies in Humanism*: J. W. Mackail. *London Mercury*, 38 (June 1938), 187.

136. *Introduction to English Literature, Volume II. The English Renaissance, 1510-1688*: Vivian de Sola Pinto; *Introduction to English Literature, Volume IV. The Victorians and After, 1830-1914*: Bonamy Dobree and Edith Batho. *Sunday Times* (July 10, 1938), p. 8.

137. *The Miltonic Setting*: E. M. W. Tillyard. *Criterion*, 17 (July 1938), 738-40.

138. *Mohammed*: Essad Bey, H. L. Ripperger, trans. *Sunday Times* (August 14, 1938), p. 6.

139. *Religion in Essence and in Manifestation*: G. Van der Leeuw, J. E. Turner, trans. *Time and Tide*, 19 (August 20, 1938), 1180.

140. *Madeleine de Scudery*: Dorothy McDougall. *Sunday Times* (August 21, 1938), p. 7.

141. *From Suffering to Fulfillment*: Hermann Keyserling, Jane Marshall, trans. *Sunday Times* (September 11, 1938), p. 10.

142. *Heaven—and Earth*: J. Middleton Murry. *Sunday Times* (September 18, 1938), p. 9.

143. *Jane Austen, A "Life"*: Elizabeth Jenkins; *Jane Austen and Some Contemporaries*: Mona Wilson. *Sunday Times* (September 25, 1938), p. 9.

144. *True Humanism*: Jacques Maritain; *Solitude and Society*: Nicolas Berdyaev. *Time and Tide*, 19 (October 22, 1938), 1463-64. Reprinted in *Image* (I-A-iv-6), pp. 110-12.

145. *Cuthbert Tunstal*: Charles Sturge. *Time and Tide*, 19 (November 12, 1938), 1576-77.

146. *The English Genius*: Hugh Kingsmill, ed. *Sunday Times* (November 13, 1938), p. 13.

147. *Purgatorio*: Dante, Laurence Binyon, trans.
     London Mercury, 39 (November 1938), 84.

148. *Modes of Thought*: A. N. Whitehead. *Time and Tide*,
     19 (December 3, 1938), 1756-57.

149. *The Life of Christ*: Hall Caine. *London Mercury*,
     39 (December 1938), 235-36.

150. *The Pleasures of Literature*: J. C. Powys.
     London Mercury, 39 (January 1939), 362-63.

151. *A Popular History of the Church*: Philip Hughes;
     History of the Dogma of the Trinity: Jules Lebreton,
     S. J. *Time and Tide*, 20 (February 25, 1939),
     244-45.

152. *Rejoice in the Lamb*: Christopher Smart. *Time
     and Tide*, 20 (March 18, 1939), 344, 346.
     Reprinted in *Image* (I-A-iv-6), pp. 46-48.

153. *Films of Time*: H. W. Nevinson. *London Mercury*, 39
     (March 1939), 559-60.

154. *The Family Reunion*: T. S. Eliot. *Time and Tide*,
     20 (April 8, 1939), 450-51.

155. *Beyond Politics*: Christopher Dawson; *The Poor and
     Ourselves*: Daniel-Rops; *Christianity and Economics*:
     Lord Stamp. *Time and Tide*, 20 (April 22,
     1939), 512.

156. *Introduction to English Literature, Volume I. The
     Beginnings to Skelton*: W. L. Renwich and
     Harold Orton; *Introduction to English Literature,
     Volume V. The Present Age*: Edwin Muir.
     Sunday Times (May 7, 1939), p. 8.

157. *Old Gods Falling*: Malcolm Elwin. *Sunday Times*
     (June 4, 1939), p. 10.

158. *Moses and Monotheism*: Sigmund Freud. *Time and Tide*, 20 (June 10, 1939), 758.

159. *The Pursuit of Poetry*: Desmond Flower, ed. *Sunday Times* (June 18, 1939), p. 6.

160. *The Divine Comedy*: Dante, John D. Sinclair, trans. *Time and Tide*, 20 (June 24, 1939), 833.

161. *Present without Leave*: D'Arcy Cresswell. *Sunday Times* (July 23, 1939), p. 6.

162. *Chateaubriand*: Joan Evans; *William Wordsworth of Rydal Mount*: Frederick Beatty. *Sunday Times* (July 30, 1939), p. 7.

163. *A Poet in Parliament*: Derek Hudson. *Sunday Times* (August 13, 1939), p. 7.

164. *Here Lies Richard Brinsley Sheridan*: Kenelm Foss. *Sunday Times* (August 27, 1939), p. 6.

165. *Torquemada, Scourge of the Jews*: Thomas Hope. *Time and Tide*, 20 (September 23, 1939), 1256.

166. *Church and State*: Luigi Sturzo. *Time and Tide*, 20 (October 21, 1939), 1369-70. Reprinted in *Image* (I-A-iv-6), pp. 115-17.

167. *Men, Women and Places*: Sigrid Undset. *Sunday Times* (October 29, 1939), p. 5.

168. *Man in the Streets*: V. W. Garratt. *Sunday Times* (November 19, 1939), p. 5.

169. *Map of Love*: Dylan Thomas. *Life and Letters Today*, 23 (November, 1939), 237-39.

170. *A Pacifist in Trouble*: W. R. Inge. *Time and Tide*, 20 (December 16, 1939), 1617.

171. *Archbishop Laud*: H. R. Trevor-Roper. *Sunday Times* (January 28, 1940), p. 6.

172. *Tradition and Romanticism*: B. Ifor Evans. *Time and Tide*, 21 (February 3, 1940), 113-14.

173. *The Last Rally, A Study of Charles II*: Hilaire Belloc. *Time and Tide*, 21 (February 24, 1940), 198.

174. *The Novel and the Modern World*: David Daiches. *Time and Tide*, 21 (March 9, 1940), 254-55.

175. *The Resurrection of Christendom*: J. H. Oldham; *Europe in Travail*: J. Middleton Murry; *Education and Social Change*: Fred Clarke; *The Message of the World-Wide Church*: W. Paton; *Christianity and Justice*: O. C. Quick. *Time and Tide*, 21 (March 23, 1940), 319-20.

176. *The Delphic Oracle*: H. W. Parke. *Time and Tide*, 21 (April 6, 1940), 369-70.

177. *Passion and Society*: Denis de Rougemont, Montgomery Belgion, trans. *Time and Tide*, 21 (April 13, 1940), 394. Reprinted in *Image* (I-A-iv-6), pp. 159-61.

178. *The March of Literature*: F. M. Ford. *Theology*, 40 (April 1940), 311-13.

179. *The Testament of Friendship, The Story of Winifred Holtby*: Vera Brittain. *Theology*, 40 (April 1940), 319.

180. *Anthology*: Edith Sitwell, comp. *Life and Letters Today*, 25 (April/June 1940), 211-13.

181. *Grand Inquisitor*: Walter Starkie. *Time and Tide*, 21 (June 1, 1940), 587-88.

182. *The Terrible Crystal*: M. Chaning-Pearce;
The Fate of Modern Culture: J. V. Langmead Casserley;
God the Living and the True: D. M. MacKinnon;
Man, His Origin and Destiny: E. L. Mascall. *Time
and Tide*, 21 (June 15, 1940), 644-45.

183. *The Pattern of Freedom*: Bruce Richmond,
selector. *Time and Tide*, 21 (July 13, 1940), 736-37.

184. *The Early Christian Attitude to War*: C. St. John
Cadoux; *The War and Christian Ethics, A Symposium*.
Time and Tide, 21 (September 7, 1940), 910-11.

185. *The Idea of the Soul in Western Philosophy and
Science*: William Ellis. *Time and Tide*, 21 (September
14, 1940), 927.

186. *East Coker*: T. S. Eliot. *Time and Tide*, 21
(October 5, 1940), 990.

187. *Boethius*: Helen M. Barrett. *Dublin Review*, 207
(October 1940), 252-53.

188. *Regeneration*: Denis Saurat; *The Christ at
Chartres*: Denis Saurat. *Time and Tide*, 21 (November
2, 1940), 1067-68.

189. *Fathers and Heretics, Studies in Dogmatic
Faith*: G. L. Prestige. *Time and Tide*, 21 (November
16, 1940), 1122-23.

190. *Sacred and Profane Love*: Sacheverell Sitwell.
Time and Tide, 21 (December 14, 1940), 1233-34.

191. *Augustans and Romantics, 1689-1830*: H. P. W. Dyson
and John Butt. *Time and Tide*, 21 (December
28, 1940), 1274-75.

192. *The Weapons of a Christian*: Dom Bernard Clements; *Faith in the Dark Ages*: J. R. Barry; *This Is the Victory*: Leslie D. Weatherhead; *The Activity of God*: A. A. David; *The Kingdom of God*: C. A. Alington; *Providence and History*: J. V. Langmead Casserley. *Time and Tide*, 22 (January 25, 1941), 72-73.

193. *The Betrayal of Christ by the Churches*: J. Middleton Murry. *Dublin Review*, 208 (January 1941), 127-29.

194. *The Problem of Pain*: C. S. Lewis. *Theology*, 42 (January 1941), 62-63.

195. *The Origin of the Jesuits*: James Broderick, S. J. *Time and Tide*, 22 (March 1, 1941), 176-77. Reprinted in *Image* (I-A-iv-6), pp. 163-65.

196. *Calvinism*: A. Dakin. *Time and Tide*, 22 (March 29, 1941), 271-72. Reprinted in *Image* (I-A-iv-6), pp. 142-43.

197. *Christian Discrimination*: George Every. *Theology*, 42 (March 1941), 182-83.

198. *Noble Castle*: Christopher Hollis; *Poetry and the Modern World*: David Daiches; *The Faith in England*: A. Herbert Rees. *Time and Tide*, 22 (May 3, 1941), 365-66.

199. *From Cabin Boy to Archbishop*: Archbishop Ullathorne. *Sunday Times* (May 4, 1941), p. 3.

200. *A Treasury of the World's Great Letters*: M. Lincoln Schuster, ed. *Time and Tide*, 22 (May 24, 1941), 442-43.

201. *An Anthology of Nature Poetry*: Viola Meynell, comp. *Time and Tide*, 22 (July 5, 1941), 564-65.

202. *New Year Letter*: W. H. Auden. *Dublin Review*, 209 (July 1941), 99-101.

203. *The Mind of the Maker*: Dorothy L. Sayers; *The Recovery of the West*: Michael Roberts. *Time and Tide*, 22 (August 16, 1941), 689-90.

204. *The Life and Times of St. Leo the Great*: T. G. Jalland. *Time and Tide*, 22 (September 20, 1941), 802-03.

205. *The New Testament in Basic English*: S. H. Hooke, ed. *Theology*, 43 (September 1941), 117-18.

206. *Awake!*: W. R. Rodgers. *Dublin Review*, 209 (October 1941), 216.

207. *The Ghost of Mr. Brown*: Ashley Sampson. *Theology*, 43 (October 1941), 256.

208. *Michael Drayton and His Circle*: Bernard H. Newdigate. *Time and Tide*, 22 (November 1, 1941), 940.

209. *Forgiveness and Reconciliation*: Vincent Taylor. *Time and Tide*, 22 (December 6, 1941), 1072. Reprinted in *Image* (I-A-iv-6), pp. 140-41.

210. *The High Church Tradition*: G. W. O. Addleshaw. *Time and Tide*, 22 (December 27, 1941), 1146. Reprinted in *Image* (I-A-iv-6), pp. 121-23.

211. *Grey Eminence*: Aldous Huxley. *New English Weekly*, 20 (January 8, 1942), 103-04.

212. *The Moral Blitz*: Bernard Causton. *Time and Tide*, 23 (January 31, 1942), 100.

213. *Man's Suffering and God's Love*: J. Messner. *Dublin Review*, 210 (January 1942), 73-74.

214. *Poems of a Decade*: A. L. Rowse. *Dublin Review*, 210 (January 1942), 95.

215. *The Nature and Destiny of Man, 1. Human Nature*: Reinhold Niebuhr. *Time and Tide*, 23 (February 14, 1942), 136-37. Reprinted in *Image* (I-A-iv-6), pp. 143-46.

216. *The Screwtape Letters*: C. S. Lewis. *Time and Tide*, 23 (March 21, 1942), 245-46. Reprinted in *Time and Tide Anthology* (London: Andre Deutsch, 1956), pp. 255-57; *Mythlore*, 2 (Autumn 1970), 22.

217. *Memories of the Supernatural*: W. H. G. Holmes. *Theology*, 44 (March 1942), 181.

218. *Poetry and Prophecy*: N. K. Chadwick; *Nostradamus, Or the Future Foretold*: James Laver. *Time and Tide*, 23 (April 4, 1942), 294.

219. *A Choice of Kipling's Verse*: T. S. Eliot, ed. *Dublin Review*, 210 (April 1942), 207-08.

220. *Essays in Criticism and Research*: Geoffrey Tillotson. *Dublin Review*, 210 (April 1942), 202-03.

221. *Street Songs*: Edith Sitwell. *Dublin Review*, 210 (April 1942), 210.

222. *Elizabethan Commentary*: Hilaire Belloc. *Time and Tide*, 23 (May 9, 1942), 390.

223. *Life and the Poet*: Stephen Spender; *Beyond the 'Isms*: Olaf Stapledon; *Masters of Reality*: Una Ellis-Fermor. *Time and Tide*, 23 (May 23, 1942), 436.

224. *Walt Whitman*: Hugh l'Anson Fausset. *Britain Today*, 73 (May 1942), 26.

225. *Chariot of Wrath*: G. Wilson Knight. *Time and Tide*, 23 (June 20, 1942), 508.

226. *La Grant Ystoire de Monsignor Tristan Li Bret*: F. C. Johnson, ed. *Time and Tide*, 23 (July 18, 1942), 581-82. Reprinted in *Image* (I-A-iv-6), pp. 183-85.

227. *Collected Poems*: Walter de la Mare. *Dublin Review*, 211 (July 1942), 185-86.

228. *The Screwtape Letters*: C. S. Lewis. *Dublin Review*, 211 (July 1942), 170-71.

229. *Mortal Strife*: J. C. Powys. *New English Weekly*, 21 (September 10, 1942), 169-70.

230. *A Life of Shakespeare*: Hesketh Pearson. *Time and Tide*, 23 (September 19, 1942), 743-44.

231. *Catholic Art and Culture*: E. J. Watkin; *The Mind of a Poet*: Raymond Dexter Havens; *An Anthology of Religious Verse*: Norman Nicholson, ed. *Time and Tide*, 23 (October 10, 1942), 804-05.

232. *Good and Evil Spirits, A Study of the Jewish and Christian Doctrine, Its Origins and Development*: Edward Langton. *Theology*, 45 (October 1942), 232-34.

233. *The Confessions of an Octogenarian*: L. P. Jacks. *Britain Today*, 78 (October 1942), 26.

234. *Catholicism and English Literature*: Edward Hutton. *Spectator*, 169 (November 20, 1942), 486.

235. *For Hilaire Belloc, Essays in Honour of His Seventy-second Birthday*: Douglas Woodruff. *Time and Tide*, 23 (November 28, 1942), 952-54.

236. *The Romantics, An Anthology*: Geoffrey Grigson,
     selector. *Time and Tide*, 23 (December 26, 1942),
     1045-46.

237. *Stone Men of Malekula*: John Layard. *Time and
     Tide*, 24 (January 16, 1943), 50-52.

238. *For Hilaire Belloc*: Douglas Woodruff, ed.
     Dublin Review, 212 (January 1943), 85-87.

239. *Wife to Mr. Milton*: Robert Graves. *Time and Tide*,
     24 (February 27, 1943), 168.

240. *God and Evil*: C. E. M. Joad. *Time and Tide*,
     24 (March 13, 1943), 211-12.

241. *The Virgin Birth in History and Faith*: Douglas Edwards.
     Time and Tide, 24 (April 3, 1943), 276.

242. *Spirit of Flame, A Study of St. John of the Cross*:
     E. Allison Peers, S. C. M.; *Donne, A Spirit
     in Conflict*: Evelyn Hardy. *Time and Tide*, 24 (April
     10, 1943), 299.

243. *Hardy the Novelist*: Lord David Cecil. *Time
     and Tide*, 24 (May 8, 1943), 380.

244. *Season and Festival*: Herbert Palmer; *Selected Poems*:
     John Hall, Keith Douglas, and Norman
     Nicholson; *Selected Poems*: Herman Melville,
     William Plomer, ed. *Time and Tide*, 24 (June 12,
     1943), 484.

245. *A Poet's Notebook*: Edith Sitwell. *Time and Tide*, 24
     (June 26, 1943), 524-25.

246. *Christianity According to St. John*: W. F. Howard;
     The Christian Failure: Charles Singer. *Time
     and Tide*, 24 (July 24, 1943), 614-15. Reprinted
     in *Image* (I-A-iv-6), pp. 87-89.

247. *Essays on the Medieval German Love Lyrics*: M. F. Richey. *Dublin Review*, 213 (July 1943), 94-96.

248. *Human Destiny*: Reinhold Niebuhr. *Time and Tide*, 24 (August 14, 1943), 668.

249. *Time, the Refreshing River*: Joseph Needham. *Time and Tide*, 24 (August 28, 1943), 704-05.

250. *The Traveller's Journey Is Done*: Dilys Powell. *Time and Tide*, 24 (September 25, 1943), 786.

251. *He Who Is, A Study in Traditional Theism*: E. L. Mascall. *Time and Tide*, 24 (October 9, 1943), 828.

252. *The Fortunes of Falstaff*: J. D. Wilson. *Time and Tide*, 24 (October 23, 1943), 869-70. Reprinted in *Image* (I-A-iv-6), pp. 40-42.

253. *Renascence*: Nicodemus. *Dublin Review*, 213 (October 1943), 192-93.

254. *Petrarch and the Renascence*: J. H. Whitfield. *Time and Tide*, 24 (November 6, 1943), 907-08.

255. *Greek Fire*: Andre Michalopoulos; *Miracle in Hellas*: Betty Wason; *Greece Fights On*: Symmachos. *Time and Tide*, 24 (December 11, 1943), 1024, 1026.

256. *Redeeming the Time*: Jacques Maritain. *Time and Tide*, 24 (December 25, 1943), 1066. Reprinted in *Image* (I-A-iv-6), pp. 161-63.

257. *Prophets for a Day of Judgment*: A. E. Baker. *Time and Tide*, 25 (February 26, 1944), 180.

258. *Paradiso*: Dante, Laurence Binyon, trans. *Britain Today*, 95 (March 1944), 26-27.

259. *Roman Vergil*: W. Jackson Knight. *Time and Tide*, 25 (April 1, 1944), 289-90. Reprinted in *Image* (I-A-iv-6), pp. 123-26.

260. *The English Bible*: Sir Herbert Grierson: *The Bible, Its Letter and Spirit*: W. C. Dick. *Time and Tide*, 25 (May 6, 1944), 400-01.

261. *Twickenham Edition of the Poems, Volumes II, IV, V*: Alexander Pope. *Time and Tide*, 25 (May 27, 1944), 466-68. Reprinted in *Image* (I-A-iv-6), pp. 42-45.

262. *St. Augustine's Confessions*: F. J. Sheed, trans.; *The Incarnation of the Word of God*: A Religious, trans. *Time and Tide*, 25 (June 24, 1944), 556. Reprinted in *Image* (I-A-iv-6), pp. 89-91.

263. *Shakespeare and the Popular Dramatic Tradition*: S. L. Bethell. *Time and Tide*, 25 (July 8, 1944), 598. Reprinted in *Image* (I-A-iv-6), pp. 37-39.

264. *Hated Servants*: H. F. Rubinstein. *Time and Tide*, 25 (July 15, 1944), 624.

265. *Milton, Man and Thinker*: Denis Saurat. *Spectator*, 173 (August 18, 1944), 154.

266. *The Trial of Harry Dobkin*: C. Bechhofer Roberts. *Time and Tide*, 25 (August 26, 1944), 748.

267. *The Battle for Britain in the Fifth Century*: T. D. Reed. *Time and Tide*, 25 (September 16, 1944), 817.

268. *We Have Been Friends Together*: Raïssa Maritain. *Time and Tide*, 25 (October 28, 1944), 946-47.

269. *The Divine Realm*: E. Lampert. *Time and Tide*, 25 (December 2, 1944), 1062.

270. *Season and Festival*: Herbert Palmer.
Poetry London, 2 (December 1944), 245-46.

271. *A Critical History of English Poetry*: H. J. C. Grierson
and J. C. Smith. *Time and Tide*, 26 (January
20, 1945), 58.

272. *Gerard Manley Hopkins*: W. H. Gardner. *Time
and Tide*, 26 (February 3, 1945), 102-03.
Reprinted in *Image* (I-A-iv-6), pp. 48-51.

273. *The Divine Realm*: Evgueny Lampert. *Theology*,
48 (February 1945), 41-42.

274. *The Rights of Man*: Jacques Maritain. *Time
and Tide*, 26 (March 24, 1945), 253-54. Reprinted
in *Image* (I-A-iv-6), pp. 113-15.

275. *Shakespeare's History Plays*: E. M. W. Tillyard.
Time and Tide, 26 (April 14, 1945), 314-15.

276. *The Children of Light and the Children of Darkness*:
Reinhold Niebuhr. *Time and Tide*, 26 (May
5, 1945), 376.

277. *Romanticism Comes of Age*: Owen Barfield.
New English Weekly, 27 (May 10, 1945),
33-34.

278. *The Trial of R. S. Buckfield*: C. E. Bechhofer Roberts,
ed. *Time and Tide*, 26 (May 19, 1945), 421.

279. *From Virgil to Milton*: C. M. Bowra. *Time and
Tide*, 26 (May 26, 1945), 439-40.

280. *Beyond Personality*: C. S. Lewis; *Light of Christ*:
Evelyn Underhill. *Time and Tide*, 26 (June 16, 1945),
506.

281. *The Arbitration, The Entrepontes of Menander*:
Menander, Gilbert Murray, trans. *Britain Today*, 111 (July 1945), 42.

282. *From Virgil to Milton*: C. M. Bowra. *Britain Today*, 112 (August 1945), 40-41.

283. *Poems from the Greek Anthology*: Forrest Reid, trans. *Poetry London*, 3 (September/October 1947), 51.

E. Edited Works

1. *Poems of Home and Overseas*. Comp. Charles Williams and V. H. Collins. Oxford: Clarendon Press, 1921, 160 pp., reissued in 1930, 216 pp.

2. *A Book of Victorian Narrative Verse*. Chosen and introduced by Charles Williams. Oxford: Clarendon Press, 1927, rpt. 1931. 325 pp.

3. *The Oxford Book of Regency Verse*. Ed. Humphrey S. Milford in collaboration with Charles Williams. Oxford: Clarendon Press, 1928. 887 pp.

4. *A Short Life of Shakespeare with Sources*. Abridged by Charles Williams from Sir Edmund Chambers's *William Shakespeare: A Study of Facts and Problems*. London: Oxford University Press, 1933, rpt. 1956. 260 pp.

5. *The Ring and the Book* by Robert Browning. The story retold by Charles Williams. London: Oxford University Press, 1934. 120 pp.

6. *The New Book of English Verse*. Ed. Charles Williams. London: V. Gollancz, 1935; New York: Macmillan, 1936. 828 pp.

7. *The Story of the Aeneid*. Retold by Charles Williams. London: Oxford University Press, 1936. 168 pp.

8. *The Passion of Christ: Being the Gospel and Narrative
   of the Passion with Short Passages Taken from
   the Saints and Doctors of the Church.* Ed. Charles
   Williams. London: Oxford University Press, 1939.
   75 pp.

9. *The New Christian Year.* Chosen by Charles Williams.
   London: Oxford University Press, 1941, rpt. 1958.
   281 pp.
   Daily devotions.

10. *The Letters of Evelyn Underhill.* Ed. Charles
    Williams. London: Longmans, Green and Company,
    1943, rpt. 1944, 1956. 343 pp.

11. *Solway Ford and Other Poems* by Wilfrid Gibson.
    A selection made by Charles Williams. London:
    Faber and Faber, 1945. 74 pp.

II. Works About Williams

A. Books

1. Hadfield, Alice Mary. *Introduction to Charles Williams*. London: Robert Hale, 1959. 221 pp.

   Mainly biographical. Events in Williams's life serve as an introduction to his thought. Williams's personal comments to the author are used to clarify certain of his concepts.

2. Shideler, Mary McDermott. *The Theology of Romantic Love: A Study in the Writings of Charles Williams*. New York: Harper, 1962; Grand Rapids, Michigan: William B. Eerdmans, 1966. 243 pp.

   The best of the treatments of Williams's theology. Part I explores Williams's method of imagery and a key image, the figure of Beatrice. Part II presents Williams's formulation of the theology of romantic love in relation to certain Christian doctrines. The last part treats the implications of this theology. A partial bibliography of Williams's works is included.

B. Articles, Chapters, and Dissertations

1. Adams, Robert Martin. *Ikon: John Milton and the Modern Critics*. Ithaca, New York: Cornell University Press, 1955. P. 222.

   Simply mentions Williams in connection with Lewis and their defense of Milton.

2. Allan, Jim. Letter. *Mythlore*, 2 (Winter 1972), 28-30.

   Remarks on the etymology and on the literary uses of the term *Logres*. The letter also touches upon related terms.

3. Allot, Kenneth. "Charles Williams." *Penguin Anthology of Contemporary Verse*. Harmondsworth, England: Penguin, 1950. Pp. 71-72.

   Comments that Williams's poems are a literary oddity and that one is included because of his influence on Eliot, Auden, and Anne Ridler.

4. Amis, Kingsley. *New Maps of Hell: A Survey of Science Fiction*. New York: Harcourt, Brace, and Company, 1960. P. 82.

   Charles Williams and C. S. Lewis are mentioned in connection with fantasy novels.

5. Anonymous. "Lines on the Reverend's Black Beard, Begun 29 June Anno Domini 1965 at the Request of His Lady-Love." *Mythlore*, 2 (Autumn 1970), 21.

   A poem on a Charles Williams character.

6. Auden, W. H. "Charles Williams: A Review Article." *The Christian Century*, 73 (May 2, 1956), 552-54.

   A general article, concentrating special attention on the novels.

7. ———. "Introduction." *The Protestant Mystics*. Ed.
   Anne Fremantle. Boston: Little, Brown, 1964. P. 29.

   Williams mentioned as having a characteristic Anglican
   style of piety.

8. ———. "The Martyr as Dramatic Hero." *Listener*,
   79 (January 4, 1968), 1-8; also published with three
   other lectures in *Secondary Worlds: The T. S.
   Eliot Memorial Lectures* (London: Faber and
   Faber, 1968), pp. 15-45.

   Concerns Williams's *Cranmer* (I-A-iii-5) and Eliot's *Murder
   in the Cathedral*.

9. Beaumont, Ernest. "Charles Williams and the Power
   of Eros." *Dublin Review*, 479 (Spring 1959),
   61-74.

   His particular focus is the fiction: *Descent into Hell, The Place
   of the Lion, All Hallows' Eve, The Greater Trumps* and
   Shadows of Ecstasy.

10. Bolling, Douglas Townshend. "Three Romances
    by Charles Williams." Dissertation, University
    of Iowa, 1970. *Dissertation Abstracts*, 31 (1971),
    4755A.

    Special attention given to the principle of Christian
    decorum, development of thematic statement through
    presentation of character interaction, and to the use of symbol
    and image in *Shadows of Ecstasy, Many Dimensions* and
    The Place of the Lion.

11. Borrow, Anthony. "The Affirmation of Images."
    Nine, 3 (Summer/Autumn 1952), 325-54.

    Treats the Way of Affirmation in the novels.

12. Braude, Nan. "Scion and Parnassus: Three
    Approaches to Myth." *Mythlore*, 1 (1969),
    6-8.

    Treats the approaches of Tolkien, Lewis and Williams.

13. ———. "The Two-Headed Beast: Notes toward
the Definition of Allegory." In *Mythcon I: Proceedings*,
ed. Glen GoodKnight, pp. 32-35. Los Angeles:
Mythopoeic Society, 1971.

> Suggests Williams's novels represent a successful
> attempt to use allegorism as a "mode of expression."

14. Brown, Robert McAfee. "Charles Williams:
Lay Theologian." *Theology Today*, 10 (July 1953),
212-29.

> Concerned with Williams's themes.

15. Bush, Douglas. *"Paradise Lost" in Our Time: Some
Comments*. New York: Peter Smith, 1948.
P. 25.

> Mentions Williams's having written a defense of Milton.

16. Carmichael, Douglas. "Love and Rejection in
Charles Williams." *Universitas*, 2 (1964),
14-22.

17. Carter, Lin. *Tolkien: A Look behind "The Lord of
the Rings."* New York: Ballantine Books,
1969. Pp. 16-20.

> Brief comments on the Inklings. Tolkien's denial of any
> influence from Williams is quoted.

18. Cavaliero, Glen. "Charles Williams on *Taliessin
through Logres*." *Gnomon*, 1 (Fall 1965), 37-45.

> An explanation of certain details in the *Taliessin*
> (I-A-i-6) cycle.

19. ———. "The Way of Affirmation: A Study of the
Writings of Charles Williams." *Church
Quarterly Review*, 157 (January/March 1956),
19-28.

20. Chandler, John Herrick. "Charles Williams, the Poet of the Co-Inherence." Dissertation. University of Chicago, 1964.

21. Christopher, J. R. "Considering *The Great Divorce.*" In *Mythcon I: Proceedings,* ed. Glen GoodKnight, pp. 40-48; and *Mythcon II: Proceedings,* ed. Glen GoodKnight, pp. 12-21. Los Angeles: Mythopoeic Society, 1971, 1972.

    Points out the similarities to Williams's *All Hallows' Eve* (I-A-ii-7).

22. Cockshut, A. O. J. "Conquest's 'The Art of the Enemy.' " *Essays in Criticism,* 7 (July 1957), 339-40.

    Criticism of the image of Williams presented by Conquest (II-B-23).

23. Conquest, Robert. "The Art of the Enemy." *Essays in Criticism,* 7 (January 1957), 42-55.

    Concerned with Williams's system of beliefs with examples from the lyric cycle. This critical piece evoked several responses from adherents of Williams.

24. ———. " 'The Art of the Enemy': Reply." *Essays in Criticism,* 7 (July 1957), 341-43.

    Answer to criticisms of his earlier piece (II-B-23).

25. Craig, Alec. "Conquest's 'The Art of the Enemy.' " *Essays in Criticism,* 7 (July 1957), 340-41.

    Endorsement of Conquest's view of Williams (II-B-23).

26. Crowley, C. P. "The Grail Poetry of Charles Williams." *University of Toronto Quarterly,* 25 (July 1956), 484-93.

27. ―――. "The Structural Pattern of Charles
Williams' *Descent into Hell.*" *Papers of the Michigan
Academy of Science, Arts, and Letters,* 39
(1954), 421-28.

Attributes the unity of the novel to Williams's creation of a
mythical pattern and symbol of the City.

28. Davidson, Clifford. "Charles Williams and
Religious Drama." *Religious Theatre* (Florida
Presbyterian College), 5 (October 1967),
121-23.

Points out that Williams uses dramatic techniques out
of fashion since the sixteenth century. Several of his dramas
resemble the medieval cycle plays in structure. Says
Williams's propaganda is the "result of his consummate
art."

29. ―――. "Williams' *All Hallows' Eve*: The Way of
Perversity." *Renascence,* 20 (Winter 1968), 86-93.

Character of Simon emphasized.

30. Davies, R. T. "Charles Williams and Romantic
Experience." *Ètudes Anglaises,* 8 (October/December
1955), 289-98.

Indicates the weakness of the theme is the reconciliation
of eros and agape, which cannot be achieved.

31. Dawson, Lawrence Russell. "Charles Williams as
Reviewer and Reviewed." Dissertation,
University of Michigan, 1960. *Dissertation Abstracts,*
20 (1960), 4659.

He discusses Williams's essay-reviews as important
sources of information about co-inherence, the
poetic crisis, the image of the City and Romantic theology.

32. ―――. "Checklist of Reviews by Charles Williams."
Papers of the Bibliographical Society of America,
55 (April/June 1961), 100-17.

33. Dawson, Lawrence R., Jr. "Reflections of Charles Williams on Fiction." Ball State Teachers College *Forum*, 5 (Winter 1964), 23-29.

    Connects the fiction Williams wrote with that he reviewed (primarily detective fiction).

34. Diggle, Margaret. "The Mathematics of the Soul." *Poetry London*, 3 (September/October 1947), 46-49.

    The appeal of geometric figures and numbers as images and Williams's use of them.

35. Dowie, William John, Jr. "Religious Fiction in a Profane Time: Charles Williams, C. S. Lewis and J. R. R. Tolkien." Dissertation, Brandeis, 1970. *Dissertation Abstracts*, 31 (1970), 2911A.

    Detective stories became a metaphor for Williams's vision of the world.

36. Dunn, Stephen P. "Mr. White, Mr. Williams, and the Matter of Britain." *Kenyon Review*, 24 (Spring 1962), 363-71.

    Williams's lyric cycle is a focus.

37. Eliot, T. S. "The Significance of Charles Williams." *Listener*, 36 (December 19, 1946), 894-95.

    Eliot concentrates on the novels.

38. Ellwood, Gracia Fay. "The Return to the Past in Williams and Eliade." In *Mythcon II: Proceedings*, ed. Glen GoodKnight, pp. 26-28. Los Angeles: Mythopoeic Society, 1972.

    The details of the returns to past time in *Descent into Hell* (I-A-ii-6), *Nights at Serampore*, and a nonfiction work are compared.

39. Engel, Claire-Eliane. "Charles Williams: Un
    Mystique Protestant." *Reforme*, No. 275 (June
    24, 1950), p. 7.

    The lyric cycle receives most of the attention; there
    are some comments on the novels. In French.

40. Evans, David W. "T. S. Eliot, Charles Williams,
    and the Sense of the Occult." *Accent*, 14
    (Spring 1954), 148-55.

    Discusses the use of the occult in Williams's novels.

41. Every, George. "Charles Williams—I. The
    Accuser." *Theology*, 51 (March 1948),
    95-100.

    This and the following article deal with thematic matters.

42. ———. "Charles Williams—II. The City and the
    Substitutions." *Theology*, 51 (April 1948),
    145-50.

43. ———. *Poetry and Personal Responsibility*. London:
    SCM Press, 1949.

    Chapters 1 and 4 concern Williams.

44. Fairchild, Hoxie Neale. *Religious Trends in
    English Poetry: Volume V: 1880-1920: Gods of a
    Changing Poetry*. New York and London:
    Columbia University Press, 1962. Pp. 260-67, 268,
    271, 279.

    Deals with the early poetry—its exploration of love,
    sex, and the Positive Way.

45. ———. *Religious Trends in English Poetry: Volume VI:
    1920-1965: Valley of Dry Bones*. New York
    and London: Columbia University Press, 1968.
    Pp. 122-24, 174, 290, 296-99, 439, 440, 444 and
    note, 482-87, 496.

In several sections she deals with the themes of the
Arthurian cycle (pp. 122-24, 290, 296-99, 440, 482-87). Also
mentions Williams in connection with Hopkins, Auden,
Eliot, and David Jones.

46. Foster, Robert. "The Heroic in Middle-Earth." In
    Mythcon II: Proceedings, ed. Glen GoodKnight,
    pp. 22-25. Los Angeles: Mythopoeic
    Society, 1972.

    Mentions *Greater Trumps* (I-A-ii-4) and *War in Heaven*
    (I-A-ii-1) in notes.

47. Fuller, Edmund. "Many Dimensions: The
    Images of Charles Williams." *Books with Men
    behind Them*. New York: Random House, 1962.
    Pp. 197-234.

    Fuller is most concerned with the novels and Williams's vision
    of the Christian image of man. Williams also mentioned
    on pp. 139-42, 13, 14, 53.

48. ———. "Charles Williams' *All Hallows' Eve*."
    Religious Dimensions in Literature. New York:
    Seabury Press, 1967. 31 pp.

    Discussion of the interpenetration of natural and supernatural
    worlds, substituted love and the holiness of all things.

49. ———. *Man in Modern Fiction: Some Minority Opinions
    on Contemporary American Writing*. New York:
    Random House, 1949. Pp. xvii, 50, 59, 62,
    79, 118.

    References to Charles Williams as a Christian writer.

50. ———. "Speaking of Books." *New York Times
    Book Review* (January 12, 1964), p. 2.

    Refers to Williams as one of England's three greatest
    contemporary masters of fantasy.

51. Fullman, Christopher Edward. "The Mind and Art of Charles Williams: A Study of His Poetry, Plays, the Novels." Dissertation, University of Wisconsin, 1955.

52. Gardner, Helen. "A Reading of *Paradise Lost.*" Oxford: Clarendon Press, 1965. Also printed in *Essays and Studies* I (1948) and *Elizabethan Drama: Modern Essays in Criticism*, ed. Ralph J. Kaufmann (1961). Pp. vii, 13, 57, 99-100, 118-20.

    References to Williams's readings of Milton. At one point she accuses Williams of an anachronism and a forcing of Milton's text (p. 57).

53. Gibb, Jocelyn, ed. *Light on C. S. Lewis.* London: Geoffrey Bles, 1965.

    Williams is mentioned on the following pages: p. 63 in "The Approach to English" by Nevill Coghill; p. 82 in "The Tutor and the Scholar" by John Lawlor; p. 112 in "Impact on America" by Chad Walsh.

54. Gigrich, John P. "An Immortality for Its Own Sake: A Study of the Concept of Poetry in the Writings of Charles Williams." Dissertation, Catholic University, Washington, 1953.

55. Göller, Karl H. "King Arthur and the Grail in the Poetry of Charles Williams." *Lebende Antike: Symposion für Rudolf Sühnel.* Berlin: Erich Schmidt, 1967. Pp. 489-501.

    Believes Williams to be the most successful in recreating and remodeling the Arthurian myth. Excellent treatment of Williams's departures and basic ideas.

56. GoodKnight, Glen. "Affirming the Images." *Mythlore*, 2 (Autumn 1970), 3.

    Dedication of the issue to Charles Williams study.

57. ———. "A Comparison of Cosmological Geography in the Works of J. R. R. Tolkien, C. S. Lewis and Charles Williams." *Mythlore*, 1 (1969), 18-22.

58. ———. "The Social History of the Inklings, J. R. R. Tolkien, C. S. Lewis and Charles Williams." *Mythlore*, 2 (Winter 1970), 7-9.

Williams said to be a catalyst in the group.

59. ———. "Transcending the Images: Archaisms and Alternatives." In *Mythcon II: Proceedings*, ed. Glen GoodKnight, pp. 3-5, 25. Los Angeles: Mythopoeic Society, 1972.

Ways of Affirmation and Negation as Williams defined them, in connection with Mythcon.

60. ———."The White Tree." In *Mythcon I: Proceedings*, ed. Glen GoodKnight, pp. 56-59. Los Angeles: Mythopoeic Society, 1971.

Reference to Williams's Broceliande.

61. Hadfield, Alice M. "Coinherence, Substitution and Exchange in Charles Williams' Poetry and Poetry-Making." *Imagination and the Spirit: Essays in Literature and the Christian Faith Presented to Clyde S. Kilby*. Ed. Charles A. Huttar. Grand Rapids, Michigan: William B. Eerdmans, 1971. Pp. 229-58. Appendix with selections from the poetry of Charles Williams, pp. 250-58.

62. Hadfield, Alice Mary. "The Relationship of Charles Williams' Working Life to His Fiction." *Shadows of Imagination: The Fantasies of C. S. Lewis, J. R. R. Tolkien, and Charles Williams*. Ed. Mark R. Hillegas. Carbondale: Southern Illinois University Press, 1969. Pp. 125-38.

Focuses on the use of office experience and knowledge

of London to make the novels more realistic. Also
comments on Williams as a person and as a staff
member (Oxford University Press).

63. Hamilton, George Rostrevor. *Hero or Fool: A Study
    of Milton's Satan.* London: G. Allen and
    Unwin, 1944. Pp. 7, 13, 21, 29, 40.

    Refutes the views of Williams and Lewis.

64. Hannay, Margaret. "C. S. Lewis Collection at
    Wheaton College." *Mythlore*, 2 (Winter 1972), 20.

    Brief description of the collection, including comments
    about Williams's letters to his wife (1939–1945), which
    have been acquired for the collection.

65. Hanshell, H. D. "Charles Williams: A Heresy
    Hunt." *The Month*, 9 (January 1953), 14-25.

    Feels there is a constant vein of self-deception in
    Williams's work. Deals with the interpretation of Dante.

66. Hartley, L. P. "The Novels of Charles Williams."
    Time and Tide, 28 (June 14, 1947), 628-30.

67. Heath-Stubbs, John. "The Arthurian Myth."
    Tribune (London, December 24, 1948), pp. 16-17.

68. ———. *Charles Williams.* British Writers and Their Work
    Series, No. 63. London: Longmans, Green,
    1955. 44 pp.

    Asserts that the Arthurian poetry appears to be Williams's
    major accomplishment and should be approached
    through Williams's concept of the poet's experience and
    its relation to spiritual truth. Influences upon Williams and
    his influence upon others as well as critical evaluation
    are the primary concerns of this work.

69. ———. "Charles Williams." *The Wind and the
    Rain*, 3 (Spring 1946), 86-88.

    A brief evaluation of the poems and plays on the occasion
    of Williams's death.

70. ———. "Charles Williams: Spiritual Power and Its Temptations." *Time and Tide*, 29 (May 1, 1948), 451-52.

The theme of power in the novels is the focus.

71. ———. "The Poetic Achievement of Charles Williams." *Poetry London*, 4 (September 1947), 42-45.

72. ———. "A Polarity: Review of *Living in Time* by Kathleen Raine and *Poems 1933-45* by Rayner Heppenstall." *Poetry London*, 3 (November/December 1947), 37-38.

Charles Williams's poetry is mentioned.

73. ———. "The Posthumous Career of Charles Williams." *New Republic*, 154 (June 11, 1966), 19-21.

His comments center on the lyric cycle.

74. Heppenstall, Rayner. "The Works of Charles Williams." *New Statesman and Nation*, 37 (May 21, 1949), 532.

Comments that Williams showed undisciplined gifts, his poems being wordy, technically uneven, and lacking in images. Additionally the human situations in his novels are said to be tenuous and unliveable.

75. Hillegas, Mark R. "Introduction." *Shadows of Imagination: The Fantasies of C. S. Lewis, J. R. R. Tolkien, and Charles Williams*. Ed. Mark Hillegas. Carbondale: Southern Illinois University Press, 1969. Pp. xiii-xix.

General comments on the fantasists.

76. Hines, Joyce R. "Getting Home: A Study of Fantasy and the Spiritual Journey in the Christian Supernatural Novels of Charles Williams and George MacDonald." Dissertation,

C.U.N.Y, 1972. *Dissertation Abstracts International,* 33 (August 1972), 755A-756A.

Defining similarities of Williams and George MacDonald as parabolists and a comparison of MacDonald's fantasy novels and Williams's seven novels.

77. Howard, Thomas T. "Charles Williams' Experiment in the Novel." Dissertation, New York University, 1970. *Dissertation Abstracts,* 31 (1970), 1760A.

Says Williams's technique derives from moral and metaphysical categories under which he understood human experience.

78. Huttar, Charles A. "Charles Williams, Novelist and Prophet." *Gordon Review* (Massachusetts), 10 (Winter 1969), 51-75.

79. Iman, Syed Mehdi. "Charles Williams: Cosmic Love." *The Poetry of the Invisible: An Interpretation of the Major English Poets from Keats to Bridges.* London: Allen and Unwin, 1937. Pp. 178-93.

Comments on love in Williams's early poetry. More quotations and enthusiasm than interpretation.

80. Ingraham, Vernon Leland. "The Verse Drama of Charles Williams." Dissertation, University of Pennsylvania, 1965. *Dissertation Abstracts,* 26 (1966), 7318.

An examination of the major themes in Williams's works and a consideration of Williams's artistic progress.

81. Irwin, W. R. "Christian Doctrine and the Tactics of Romance: The Case of Charles Williams." *Shadows of Imagination: The Fantasies of C. S. Lewis, J. R. R. Tolkien, and Charles Williams.* Ed.

Mark Hillegas. Carbondale: Southern Illinois
University Press, 1969. Pp. 139-49.

Discusses the interplay of narrative and doctrine, art
and rhetoric in the romances, dwelling on the abuse of power,
order and the use of myth.

82. ———. "There and Back Again: The Romances of
Williams, Lewis, and Tolkien." *Sewanee
Review*, 69 (Autumn 1961), 566-78.

83. Jones, David. "The Arthurian Legend: A Study
of the Posthumous Fragments by Charles
Williams." *The Tablet*, 192 (December 25, 1948),
419-21.

Discussion of the material in *Arthurian Torso* (I-A-iv-5) by a poet
working in the same area.

84. Kawano, Roland M. "The Impact of Charles
Williams' Death on C. S. Lewis." *Mythcon I:
Proceedings*. Ed. Glen GoodKnight, pp. 27-28.
Los Angeles: Mythopoeic Society, 1971.

Recounts, briefly, the friendship, emphasizing the Inklings.

85. Kilby, Clyde S. *The Christian World of C. S. Lewis*.
Appleford, Abington, Berkshire: Marcham Manor
Press, 1965; Grand Rapids, Michigan:
William B. Eerdmans, 1965. Pp. 48n, 64, 80n,
97n, 111-12, 193, 197, 198-200, 201,
203-04, 205, 206.

Mentioned is Williams's influence upon Lewis.

86. ———. "Tolkien, Lewis, and Williams." In
Mythcon I: Proceedings, ed. Glen GoodKnight,
pp. 3-4. Los Angeles: Mythopoeic Society,
1971.

Concentrates on the friendships; discusses Lewis's evaluation
of Williams's works.

87. King, James Roy. "Christian Fantasy in the
    Novels of C. S. Lewis and Charles Williams."
    Journal of Religious Thought, 11 (Autumn/Winter
    1953-1954), 46-60.

    Suggests that the fantasies of Williams and Lewis
    fulfill a basic need for fantasy. Uses Herbert Read's
    three-fold characterization of fantasy in the
    discussion.

88. Kreeft, Peter. *C. S. Lewis*. Contemporary Writers
    in Christian Perspective. Grand Rapids,
    Michigan: William B. Eerdmans, 1969. P. 4.

    Williams is listed as one of the influences on Lewis.

89. Kuhl, Rand. "Owen Barfield in Southern
    California." *Mythlore*, 1 (1969), 8-10.

    Williams is mentioned in connection with the Affirmation of
    Images and Romantic Love.

90. La Lande, Sister M. "Williams' Pattern of
    Time in *Descent into Hell*." *Renascence*, 15 (Winter
    1963), 88-95.

    One of Williams's time schemes follows the Platonic
    notion of time as constant emergence; the other,
    the Augustinian notion of time divided by "now," time
    being the link between now and the eternal.

91. *Letters of James Agee to Father Flye*. New York:
    George Braziller, 1962. P. 203.

    Comments on Williams's gift for conveying borderline states
    of mind or being.

92. Lewis, C. S. "Preface." *Essays Presented to
    Charles Williams*. Ed. C. S. Lewis. London: Oxford
    University Press, 1947; Grand Rapids,
    Michigan: William B. Eerdmans, 1966.

    General biographical and critical information, praise of
    Williams's work.

93. ———. "To Charles Williams." *Poems*. Ed.
    Walter Hooper. London: Geoffrey Bles, 1964;
    New York: Harcourt Brace, 1965. P. 105.

    Revision of a poem appearing in *Britain Today* (August 1945,
    p. 14), on the death of Charles Williams.

94. ———. "Williams and the Arthuriad." *Arthurian
    Torso*. London: Oxford University Press, 1948.

    Lewis offers interpretations of the obscure poetry and
    a systematic outline for the poems. Indispensable.

95. Lewis, W. H., ed. *Letters of C. S. Lewis*. London:
    Geoffrey Bles, 1966; New York: Harcourt,
    Brace and World, 1966.

    Williams is mentioned on pages 168, 169, 177, 195, 196-97,
    206, 208, 212, 222, 244, 269, 287-88.

96. Linden, William. Letter. *Mythlore*, 2 (Winter
    1970), 21.

    Objects to "Cosmological Geography" (II-B-57)
    on grounds of a distortion of Williams.

97. Lindskoog, Kathryn. "Farewell to Shadowlands:
    C. S. Lewis on Death." In *Mythcon I:
    Proceedings*, ed. Glen GoodKnight, pp. 10-12.
    Los Angeles: Mythopoeic Society, 1971.

    Revised form appears in *C. S. Lewis: Mere Christian* (Glendale,
    California: Regal Books, 1973). Mentions Williams's
    death.

98. Longaker, Mark and Edwin C. Bolles. *Contemporary
    English Literature*. Appleton-Century Handbooks
    of Literature. Ed. Albert C. Baugh. New
    York: Appleton Century-Crofts, 1953. P. 77.

    Includes quotations from Williams's *Poetry at
    Present* (I-A-iv-1).

99. McMichael, Barbara. "Hell Is Oneself: An Examination of the Concept of Damnation in Charles Williams' *Descent into Hell*." *Studies in the Literary Imagination*, 1 (October 1968), 59-61.

One of the best articles on *Descent into Hell* (I-A-ii-6); explores the idea of self-damnation.

100. Mason, Eugene. "Charles Williams and His Work." *Bookman*, 68 (April 1925), 26-27.

General comments on the early poetry.

101. Mathew, Gervase. "Williams and the Arthuriad." *Time and Tide*, 30 (January 1, 1949), 14.

102. Maurer, Helen. Letter. *Mythlore*, 2 (Winter 1972), 27-28.

Questions the relation of "Noises" (I-B-28) to *All Hallows' Eve* (I-A-ii-7).

103. Maynard, Theodore. "Charles Williams: Pan and Pan-Anglicanism." *Our Best Poets: English and American*. New York: Henry Holt, 1922. Pp. 29-42.

General article commenting on Williams's philosophical position and poetry.

104. ———. "The Poetry of Charles Williams." *North American Review*, 210 (September 1919), 401-11.

An enthusiastic evaluation of the early poetry, pointing to similarities between Williams's work and that of the metaphysical poets.

105. Mello Moser, Fernando de. "Charles Williams: Demanda, visão e mito." Dissertação. Lisboa: Gráfica Santelmo, 1969.

106. Moorman, Charles. *The Book of Kyng Arthur*: *The Unity of Malory's Morte d'Arthur*. Lexington, Kentucky: University of Kentucky Press, 1965. Pp. 91, 99.

Mentions Williams's interpretation and use of Malory.

107. ———. "Charles Williams." *Arthurian Triptych*. Berkeley: University of California Press, 1960. Pp. 38-101.

Chapter III is devoted wholly to Williams; two other chapters (II and VI) deal with his recasting of Arthurian myth and the relation of his work to that of C. S. Lewis and T. S. Eliot. His point is that Williams used the Arthurian myth to "exploit his entire concept of Christian life in mythopoetic terms" and to render his concepts universal.

108. ———. "Myth in the Novels of Charles Williams." *Modern Fiction Studies*, 3 (Winter 1957/1958), 321-28.

Asserts that Williams uses the mythical and the occult to introduce his themes of good and evil, order and chaos, and that the miraculous is used to set off human reactions of the characters. *Descent into Hell* (I-A-ii-6) is used as an example of Williams's use of myth.

109. ———. "Zion and Gomorrah: Charles Williams." *The Precincts of Felicity: The Augustinian City of the Oxford Christians*. Gainesville: University of Florida Press, 1966. Pp. 30-64.

The image of the City determines the tone and form of the works of these writers and their shared use of the image is the characteristic uniting them as a group.

110. Morgan, Kathleen E. "The Affirmative Way: Poetry of Charles Williams." *Christian Themes in Contemporary Poetry: A Study of English Poetry*

of the Twentieth Century. London: SCM
Press, 1965. Pp. 65-91.

Considers the Arthurian poems and their Christian themes.

111. Murray, Patrick. *Milton: The Modern Phase: A Study of Twentieth-Century Criticism.* New York: Barnes Noble, 1967. Pp. 9, 66, 70, 74, 82, 120, 130, 144*n*, 145*n*, 152, 156.

Williams's views of Milton are referred to.

112. Myers, Doris T. "Brave New World: The Status of Women According to Tolkien, Lewis, and Williams." *Cimarron Review*, 17 (October 1971), 13-19.

Williams's treatment of women differs from that of the others in that he doesn't portray women as invariably subject to men. He escaped the narrow attitudes of Lewis and Tolkien.

113. Nicholson, Norman. "Notes on the Way." *Time and Tide*, 32 (July 21, 1951), 697-98.

114. ———. "Notes on the Way." *Time and Tide*, 32 (July 28, 1951), 719.

115. Page, Frederick. "Charles Williams." *The Lantern* (Oxford University Press, January 1940), pp. 87-89.

116. ———, ed. "Charles Williams Supplement to the *Periodical*." *Periodical* (July 1945), supplement, i-iv.

Mainly quotations from obituaries.

117. Parsons, Geoffrey. "The Spirit of Charles Williams." *Atlantic Monthly*, 184 (November 1949), 77-79.

All seven novels are briefly treated but *Descent into Hell* (I-A-ii-6) and *The Place of the Lion* (I-A-ii-3) are said to be the best of the seven.

118. Patterson, Nancy-Lou. "Anti-Babels: Images
of the Divine Center in *That Hideous Strength*." In
Mythcon II: Proceedings, ed. Glen GoodKnight,
pp. 6-11. Los Angeles: Mythopoeic
Society, 1972.

Quotes a brief definition from *Figure of Beatrice* (I-A-iv-4).

119. ———. "Archetypes of the Mother in the
Fantasies of George MacDonald." In *Mythcon I:
Proceedings*, ed. Glen GoodKnight, pp. 17, 19n. Los
Angeles: Mythopoeic Society, 1971.

Williams's baptism scene in *All Hallows' Eve*
(I-A-ii-7) is mentioned.

120. Paxon, Diana. "The Holy Grail." *Mythlore*, 3
(Spring 1973), 10-11, 31.

Includes comments on *Arthurian Torso* (I-A-iv-5).

121. Peckham, Robert Wilson. "The Novels of
Charles Williams." Dissertation, University of
Notre Dame, 1965.

Analysis is twofold: a study of the *ethos* and *mythos* to
ascertain archetypal and formal affinities of each
work and an analysis of the genre of each.

122. Peoples, Galen. "The Agnostic in the Whirlwind:
The Novels of Charles Williams." *Mythlore*,
2 (Autumn 1970), 10-15.

Groups the novels and discusses the plots and themes
of each.

123. ———. "The Great Beast: Imagination in
Harness," *Mythlore*, 2 (Winter 1970),
19-20.

Discusses the potency of the imagination and likens the
unharnessed imagination to Williams's beast-archetypes in
Place of the Lion (I-A-ii-3).

124. Pitt, Valerie. "Conquest's 'The Art of the Enemy.' " *Essays in Criticism*, 7 (July 1957), 330-35.

Objections to Conquest's (II-B-23) charges of totalitarianism and perversion in Williams's works.

125. Portugal, Eustace. "Charles Williams." *Bookman*, 81 (March 1932), 314-15.

Calls Williams an intellectual adventurer. Thinks his poetry is the most successful of his works.

126. Power, Sister Mary James, S.S.N.D. "Charles Williams Sings the Mystery of Love." *Poets at Prayer*. New York: Sheed and Ward, 1938; Freeport, New York: Books for Libraries Press, 1968. Pp. 151-65.

Covers the relation of Williams and his work to the Church of England and Christianity in general.

127. Press, John. *The Chequer'd Shade*. London: Oxford University Press, 1958. Pp. 59-61.

General comments.

128. Ready, William. "The Inklings and the Myth." *The Tolkien Relation*. Chicago: Henry Regnery, 1968; New York: Warner, 1969. Pp. 19-32.

Comments on the interchanges among the group that included Williams, Tolkien and Lewis.

129. Reilly, Robert J. "Charles Williams and Romantic Theology." *Romantic Religion: A Study of Barfield, Lewis, Williams and Tolkien*. Athens, Georgia: University of Georgia Press, 1971. Pp. 148-89.

Sees the purpose of these writers as the defense of religion by traditional romantic means and the defense of romanticism by showing it to be religious.

130. ———. "Romantic Religion in the Work of
Owen Barfield, C. S. Lewis, Charles Williams,
and J. R. R. Tolkien." Dissertation, Michigan State
University, 1960. *Dissertation Abstracts*, 21 (1960),
3461-62.

See II-B-129.

131. Ridler, Anne. "Introduction." *Image of the
City and Other Essays*. London: Oxford University
Press, 1958. Pp. ix-lxxii.

Biographical details form the basis for a discussion of
the development of Williams's thought and art
and Williams's own conversational comments are frequently
used for clarification. An incomplete but helpful
bibliography included.

132. Roulet, William Matthew. "The Figure of the
Poet in the Arthurian Poems of Charles
Williams." Dissertation, St. John's University,
1965. *Dissertation Abstracts*, 28 (1965),
2694A.

Builds on Lewis's *Torso* (I-A-iv-5), studying the figure
of Taliessin in the two volumes of Arthurian
poetry.

133. Ruskin, Laura A. "Three Good Mothers:
Galadril, Psyche, and Sybil Conigsby." In *Mythcon
I: Proceedings*, ed. Glen GoodKnight, pp. 12-14.
Los Angeles: Mythopoeic Society, 1971.

"Sybil culminates the Good Mother."

134. Russell, Mariann Barbara. "The Idea of the
City of God." Dissertation, Columbia
University, 1965. *Dissertation Abstracts*, 26
(1965), 3350-3351A.

Considers the uses of allegory in the work of Williams,
Lewis, Tolkien. The City and the company in
Williams are treated.

135. Sadler, Glenn E. "Introduction to 'The Noises That Weren't There' by Charles Williams." *Mythlore*, 2 (Autumn 1970), 17.

General comments about the three chapters of typescript.

136. Sadler, Glenn Edward. "On Seeing Amen House Demolished." *Mythlore*, 2 (Autumn 1970), 6.

Poem, "For Charles Williams."

137. Sale, Roger. "England's Parnassus: C. S. Lewis, Charles Williams, and J. R. R. Tolkien." *Hudson Review*, 16 (Summer 1964), 203-25.

Stresses the Arthurian poems, concluding that Williams uses his symbols as icons (reminders of truths already believed). In Williams's work only the system to which the icons belong is clear, not the imagery.

138. Sayers, Dorothy L. "Charles Williams." *Time and Tide*, 31 (December 2, 1950), 1220.

139. ———. "Charles Williams: A Poet's Critic." *The Poetry of Search and the Poetry of Statement*. London: V. Gollancz, 1963. Pp. 69-88.

140. Sayers, Dorothy Leigh. "Dante and Charles Williams." *Christian Letters to a Post Christian World: A Selection of Essays*. Selected by Roderick Jellema. Grand Rapids, Michigan: William B. Eerdmans, 1969. Pp. 159-77.

Originally titled "Charles Williams: A Poet's Critic" (see II-B-139). Titles indicate the subject matter: correspondences between Dante and Williams.

141. Sayers, Dorothy L. "Introduction." *James I* by Charles Williams. London: Arthur Barker, 1951. Pp. ix-xii.

142. ———. "The Poetry of the Image in Dante and
Charles Williams." *Further Papers on Dante.*
London: Methuen, 1957. Pp. 183-204.

Suggests that Williams carries on the tradition of
Dante in the Affirmative Way, introducing new and fruitful
images which enrich the tradition.

143. Sellery, J'nan. "Fictive Modes in Charles
Williams' *All Hallows' Eve.*" *Genre*, 1
(October 1968), 316-31.

144. Sharpe, Eric J. "Charles Williams och den
engelska kristendomromanen." *Vår lösen*, 56 (1965),
173-78.

145. Shideler, Mary McDermott. "Are These Myths
True?" In *Mythcon II: Proceedings*, ed. Glen
GoodKnight, pp. 37-39. Los Angeles: Mythopoeic
Society, 1972.

She quotes Williams on myth several times.

146. ———. *Charles Williams: A Critical Essay.* Grand
Rapids, Michigan: William B. Eerdmans,
1969. 48 pp.

General study.

147. ———. "Excerpts from a Letter about Charles
Williams." *Mythlore*, 2 (Autumn 1970), 6.

Informal notes about reading Williams.

148. Slater, Ian Myles. "Selected Materials from a
Study of *The Worm Ouroboros.*" In *Mythcon II:
Proceedings*, ed. Glen GoodKnight, pp. 33-36.
Los Angeles: Mythopoeic Society, 1972.

Quotation from "The Figure of Arthur" (I-A-iv-5).

149. Spacks, Patricia Meyer. "Charles Williams:
The Fusions of Fiction." *Shadows of Imagination: The
Fantasies of C. S. Lewis, J. R. R. Tolkien, and
Charles Williams*. Ed. Mark R. Hillegas. Carbondale:
Southern Illinois University Press, 1969.
Pp. 150-59.

The supernatural in his novels is a bridge between the
psychological and theological, providing an objective
correlative for modes of feeling and theological truths.

150. ———. "Charles Williams: A Novelist's
Pilgrimage." *Religion in Life*, 29 (Spring 1960),
277-88.

Treatment of the novels. In *Descent into Hell* (I-A-ii-6) and
All Hallows' Eve (I-A-ii-7) she finds form and content
successfully fused; both novels utilize objective
correlative of two worlds, the living and the dead, existing
simultaneously.

151. ———. "Conquest's 'Art of the Enemy.' " *Essays
in Criticism*, 7 (July 1957), 335-39.

Objections to Conquest's (II-B-23) view of totalitarianism
in Williams's works.

152. Spanos, William V. "Charles Williams' *Judgement
at Chelmsford*: A Study in the Aesthetic of
Sacramental Time." *Christian Scholar*, 45 (Summer
1962), 107-17.

Williams's reconciliation of opposites is his major
contribution to drama. *Judgement* (I-A-iii-6) is used as an
example of Williams's concept of sacramental time;
in it, present and past are unified by the concept of eternal
present.

153. ———. "Charles Williams' 'Seed of Adam': The
Existential Flight from Death." *Christian
Scholar*, 49 (Summer 1966), 105-18.

Also appears in Spanos's *Christian Tradition in Modern
British Verse Drama* (II-B-154). The one difference in Williams's

work and recent existential pieces is Williams's
redemptive resolution; other elements are quite similar.

154. ———. *The Christian Tradition in Modern British
Verse Drama: The Poetics of Sacramental Time*. New
Brunswick, New Jersey: Rutgers University
Press, 1967. Pp. 68-80, 104-24, 155-83,
294-304.

Chapters III, IV, V and IX have sections on plays by
Williams and Williams is mentioned throughout. Plays discussed
are *Judgement at Chelmsford* (I-A-iii-6) (Chapter III,
pp. 68-80), *Thomas Cranmer of Canterbury* (I-A-iii-5) (Chapter
IV, pp. 104-24), *Seed of Adam* (I-A-iii-8, 9), *Death of
Good Fortune* (I-A-iii-8, 9), *House by the Stable* (I-A-iii-8, 9) and
Grab and Grace (I-A-iii-8, 9) (Chapter V, pp. 155-83), and
House of the Octopus (I-A-iii-9) (Chapter IX, pp. 294-304).

155. Starr, Nathan Comfort. "The Spiritual Land of
Logres." *King Arthur Today: The Arthurian
Legend in English and American Literature, 1901-1953*.
Gainesville, Florida: University of Florida
Press, 1954. Pp. 144-88.

Concentrates on Williams and the Grail legend. Also pp.
43, 137-39, 141-42, 143.

156. Thrash, Lois G. "A Source for the Redemption
Theme in *The Cocktail Party*." *Texas Studies
in Literature and Language*, 9 (Winter 1968), 547-53.

The Greater Trumps (I-A-ii-4) is cited as a source for
characters and theme in the Eliot play.

157. Thrash, Lois Glenn. "Thematic Use of the
Characters in the Novels of Charles Williams."
Dissertation, Texas Tech University, 1972.
Dissertation Abstracts, 33 (1972), 4436A.

158. Trowbridge, Clinton W. "The Beatricean
Character in the Novels of Charles Williams."
Sewanee Review, 79 (Summer 1971), 335-43.

Discusses Lester (*All Hallows' Eve* [I-A-ii-7]) and her

precursors. Lester, who offers herself up like Christ, is shown as a symbol, not just pointed out as one in the novel.

159. ———. "The Twentieth Century British Supernatural Novel." Dissertation, University of Florida, 1958. *Dissertation Abstracts*, 18 (1960), 1800.

Emphasizes Williams, Lewis, and Tolkien in his treatment of the spiritualistic-supernatural novel, the occult-supernatural novel and the "tale of terror."

160. Urang, Gunnar. "Charles Williams: Fantasy and the Ontology of Love." *Shadows of Heaven: Religion and Fantasy in the Writing of C. S. Lewis, Charles Williams, and J. R. R. Tolkien.* Philadelphia: Pilgrim Press, 1971. Pp. 51-92.

Considers Williams a sacramentalist, exploring in his article all the implications of this view. One of the best articles on the fiction of Williams.

161. Versinger, Georgette. "Charles Williams." *Ètudes Anglaises*, 18 (July/September 1965), 285-95.

General article about Williams, who is not well known in France. Article in French, quotations from English texts.

162. Wain, John. *Sprightly Running: Part of an Autobiography.* London: Macmillan, 1962. New York: St. Martin's Press, 1962, rpt. 1963, 1965. Pp. 147-52, 153-54, 181, 183, 185.

Comments on Williams concerning his lectures at Oxford.

163. Walsh, Chad. "Charles Williams' Poetry." *Poetry*, 79 (November 1951), 103-06.

Praise of Williams's imagery and his accomplishment in *Region of the Summer Stars* (I-A-i-7).

164. ———. *C. S. Lewis: Apostle to the Skeptics.* New York: Macmillan, 1949. Pp. 18, 69-70, 135-37, 156, 171.

Touches on Williams's influence through the novels.

165. Wandall, Frederick S. "Charles Williams." *Minor British Novelists.* Ed. Charles A. Hoyt. Carbondale: Southern Illinois University Press, 1967; London and Amsterdam: Feffer and Simons, 1967. Pp. 121-34.

Says Williams has no peer in the field of Christian allegory.

166. Watkins, Vernon. "Three Sonnets for Charles Williams." *The Wind and the Rain,* 7 (1951), 90-91.

The subject is the Arthurian poetry of Williams.

167. Weathers, Winston. "The Rhetoric of Certitude." *Southern Humanities Review,* 2 (Spring 1968), 213-22.

Deals with Williams's prose style, detailing the mannerisms of language on which the "rhetoric of certitude" is built.

168. Wedgwood, C. V. "Notes on the Way." *Time and Tide,* 31 (April 22, 1950), 387.

169. Weinig, Sister Mary Anthony. "Images of Affirmation: Perspectives of the Fiction of Charles Williams, C. S. Lewis, J. R. R. Tolkien." *University of Portland Review,* 20 (1968), 43-46.

Shows that the approaches of the three are different but the focus—the conflict between good and evil—is the same.

170. White, William Luther. *The Image of Man in C. S. Lewis*. Nashville and New York: Abingdon Press, 1969. Pp. 32-33, 92-93, 181, 197, 204.

Material on the Inklings and Williams's influence on Lewis.

171. Williams, Michal. "As I Remember Charles Williams." *Episcopal Churchnews*, 119 (April 12, 1953), 12-14.

By his wife.

172. Wilson, Simone. "To Michal Williams." *Mythlore*, 2 (Autumn 1970), 21.

Poem on the news of her death.

173. Winship, George Parker, Jr. "This Rough Magic: The Novels of Charles Williams." *Yale Review*, 40 (December 1950), 285-96.

Discusses the question of the genre of the novels.

174. ———. "The Novels of Charles Williams." *Shadows of Imagination: The Fantasies of C. S. Lewis, J. R. R. Tolkien, and Charles Williams*. Ed. Mark Hillegas. Carbondale: Southern Illinois University Press, 1969. Pp. 111-24.

Says the paradox of Williams's fiction is that for his fantasy he's not content with a willing suspension of disbelief. He demands the "destruction of disbelief."

175. Wright, Elizabeth. "Theology in the Novels of Charles Williams." *Stanford University Honors Essays in Humanities*, No. 5/6 (1962). Pp. 15-59.

In some catalogues listed under Kantor, Betty. *The Sin of Pride in "The Pardoner's Tale."*

176. Wright, Marjorie Evelyn. "The Cosmic Kingdom of Myth: A Study in the Myth-Philosophy of Charles Williams, C. S. Lewis, and J. R. R.

Tolkien." Dissertation, University of Illinois,
1960. *Dissertation Abstracts*, 21 (1960),
3464-65.

The three are treated together. Wright believes the desire
for cosmic order lay behind the decision of the
mythmakers to create their own cosmic kingdoms.

177. Wright, Marjorie E. "The Vision of Cosmic Order
in the Oxford Mythmakers." *Imagination and the
Spirit: Essays in Literature and the Christian Faith
Presented to Clyde S. Kilby*. Ed. Charles A.
Huttar. Grand Rapids, Michigan: William B.
Eerdmans, 1971. Pp. 259-76.

178. Zuber, Bernie. "Across the Brandywine."
Mythlore, 2 (Autumn 1970), 3.

Comments on his impression of Williams's work
read before designing a cover for this issue of *Mythlore*.

179. ———. "Across the Brandywine." *Mythlore*, 2
(Winter 1972), 10-12.

Comments on *Mythcon II* which included the
presentation of a masque based on *The Greater Trumps*
(I-A-ii-4).

180. Zylstra, Sape Anne. "Charles Williams: An
Analysis and Appraisal of His Major Work."
Dissertation, Emory University, 1969.
Dissertation Abstracts International, 30 (1969),
4468A.

Discussion of Romantic theology which rests on the
notion of two levels of reality which ideally interpenetrate
and of the images which lead the lover to the
apprehension of its ideal referent in the divine realm.

C. Reviews
(A Partial List)

i. Windows of Night (1924) [I-A-i-4]

1. Freeman, John. *London Mercury*, 13 (January 1926), 311-13.

2. Gorman, Herbert S. *New York Times Books* (June 28, 1925), p. 14.

3. Maynard, Theodore. *Saturday Review of Literature*, 2 (November 14, 1925), 294.

4. Tate, Allen. *New Republic*, 44 (October 14, 1925), 209-10.

5. Unsigned. *The Contemporary Review*, 127 (May 1925), 44-46.

6. Unsigned. *Nation and Athenaeum*, 36 (February 21, 1925), 721.

7. Unsigned. *Times Literary Supplement* (February 26, 1925), p. 135.

ii. Poetry at Present (1930) [I-A-iv-1]

1. Arns, Karl. *Zeitschrift für franzos und englische Unterricht*, 32 (1933), 48.

2. Groth, Ernst. *Anglia Beiblat*, 43 (November 1932), 341-45.

3. Martin, Christopher. *Catholic World*, 132 (January 1931), 504-05.

4. Mason, Eugene. *Bookman*, 78 (April 1930), 57-58.

5. Richards, I. A. *Yale Review*, 21 (Autumn 1931), 191-93.

6. Welby, T. Earle. *Week-End Review* (April 1, 1930), pp. 169-70.

7. Unsigned. *Nation*, 131 (November 12, 1930), 531.

8. Unsigned. *Nation and Athenaeum*, 46 (March 29, 1930), 898.

9. Unsigned. *Spectator*, 145 (July 5, 1930), 28.

10. Unsigned. *Times Literary Supplement* (March 20, 1930), p. 229.

iii. War in Heaven (1930) [I-A-ii-1]

1. Farrelly, John. *New Republic*, 121 (October 31, 1949), 20.

2. McLaughlin, Richard. *Saturday Review of Literature*, 32 (October 1, 1949), 16.

3. Nicholl, Louise Townsend. *New York Herald Tribune Books* (October 9, 1949), p. 4.

4. Unsigned. *New Yorker*, 25 (October 8, 1949), 105.

5. Unsigned. *Time*, 54 (October 10, 1949), 110.

6. Unsigned. *Times Literary Supplement* (June 12, 1930), p. 494.

iv. Many Dimensions (1931) [I-A-ii-2]

1. Breit, Harvey. *Atlantic Monthly*, 184 (September 1949), 86.

2. Farrelly, John. *New Republic*, 121 (October 31, 1949), 20.

3. McLaughlin, Richard. *Saturday Review of Literature*, 32 (September 17, 1949), 38.

4. Sayers, Dorothy L. *New York Times Books* (August 21, 1949), p. 7.

5. Sugrue, Thomas. *New York Herald Tribune Books* (August 28, 1949), p. 4.

6. Unsigned. *New Yorker*, 25 (September 17, 1949), 102.

v. The Place of the Lion (1931) [I-A-ii-3]

1. Arrowsmith, J. E. S. *London Mercury*, 25 (November 1931), 112-13.

2. Enslin, Theodore. *Crozer Quarterly*, 28 (July 1951), 278.

3. Garrigue, Jean. *New Republic*, 124 (April 23, 1951), 21.

4. Gresham, William Lindsay. *Saturday Review of Literature*, 34 (March 24, 1951), 14.

5. Hughes, Riley. *Catholic World*, 173 (May 1951), 151.

6. Loveman, Amy. *Saturday Review of Literature*, 8 (April 23, 1932), 684.

7. Stallings, Sylvia. *New York Herald Tribune Books* (March 11, 1951), p. 8.

8. Walsh, Chad. *New York Times Books* (March 11, 1951), pp. 1, 19.

9. Unsigned. *Nation*, 134 (June 8, 1932), 658.

10. Unsigned. *New York Times Books* (May 1, 1932), p. 18.

11. Unsigned. *New Yorker*, 27 (March 24, 1951), 104-05.

12. Unsigned. *Times Literary Supplement* (October 1, 1931), p. 750.

vi. Three Plays (1931) [I-A-iii-4]

1. Miller, Burgoyne. *Bookman*, 80 (July 1931), 225.

2. Unsigned. *Times Literary Supplement* (August 27, 1931), p. 644.

vii. The English Poetic Mind (1932) [I-A-iv-2]

1. Arns, Karl. *Englische Studien*, 68 (June 1933), 119-20.

2. Davis, E. C. *Modern Language Review*, 28 (January 1933), 112-13.

3. French, Yvonne. *London Mercury*, 27 (November 1933), 87.

4. Harper, George McLean. *Saturday Review of Literature*, 9 (July 23, 1932), 6.

5. Kingsmill, Hugh. *English Review*, 55 (August 1933), 210-14.

6. Maynard, Theodore. *Catholic World*, 136 (October 1932), 119-21.

7. Morley, Edith J. *Review of English Studies*, 9 (July 1933), 325-26.

8. Nicholl, Louise Townsend. *New York Herald Tribune Books* (April 9, 1950), p. 8.

9. Welby, T. Earle. *Week-End Review*, 5 (May 21, 1932), 646.

10. Wilson, R. N. D. *Spectator*, 149 (August 27, 1932), 268.

11. Unsigned. *New Statesman and Nation*, 4 (August 13, 1932), 186.

12. Unsigned. *Times Literary Supplement* (June 16, 1932), p. 443.

viii. **The Greater Trumps** (1932) [I-A-ii-4]

1. Klein, Alexander. *New Republic*, 123 (July 10, 1950), 18-19.

2. McLaughlin, Richard. *Saturday Review of Literature*. 33 (April 8, 1950), 19.

3. Nicholl, Louise Townsend. *New York Herald Tribune Books* (April 9, 1950), p. 8.

4. Trese, Leo J. *Commonweal*, 52 (May 5, 1950), 104-05.

5. Walsh, Chad. *New York Times Books* (April 9, 1950), p. 6.

6. Unsigned. *New Yorker*, 26 (April 8, 1950), 119.

7. Unsigned. *Times Literary Supplement* (May 5, 1932),
   p. 328.

8. Unsigned. *Time*, 55 (April 10, 1950), 100-02.

ix. **Shadows of Ecstasy** (1932) [I-A-ii-5]

1. Burnham, Philip. *New York Times Books* (December
   17, 1950), p. 15.

2. Garrigue, Jean. *New Republic*, 123 (November 6,
   1950), 20-21.

3. McLaughlin, Richard. *Saturday Review of Literature*,
   33 (September 23, 1950), 18.

4. Nicholl, Louise Townsend. *New York Herald
   Tribune Books* (October 8, 1950), p. 31.

5. Sandrock, Mary. *Catholic World*, 172 (December
   1950), 234.

6. Unsigned. *New Yorker*, 26 (November 11, 1950), 162.

7. Unsigned. *Times Literary Supplement* (February 16,
   1933), p. 106.

x. **Bacon** (1933) [I-A-vi-1]

1. Carswell, Donald. *New Statesman*, 6 (August 5,
   1933), 166.

2. Coblentz, Stanton A. *New York Times Books* (February
   25, 1934), p. 11.

3. Irvine, L. Lloyd. *Spectator*, 150 (June 23, 1933), 916-18.

4. McCole, Camille, *Catholic World*, 139 (June 1934), 375.

5. Mangioni, Jerre. *New Republic*, 79 (June 27, 1934), 191.

6. Powers, W. D. *Commonweal*, 19 (April 13, 1934), 669-70.

7. Pritchett, V. S. *Week-End Review*, 8 (July 8, 1934), 41.

8. Vivas, Eliseo. *Nation*, 138 (April 4, 1934), 393.

9. Initialed: H. H. C. *America*, 51 (July 28, 1934), 379.

10. Unsigned. *Christian Century*, 51 (March 7, 1934), 332.

11. Unsigned. *Times Literary Supplement* (June 8, 1933), p. 389.

xi. Reason and Beauty in the Poetic Mind (1933) [I-A-iv-3]

1. Batho, Edith C. *Review of English Studies*, 12 (April 1936), 234-36.

2. Clarke, Arthur. *New Statesman*, 7 (January 27, 1934), 128.

3. Henn, Hans Georg. *Deutsche Literaturzeitung*, 57 (May 17, 1936), 839-40.

4. Roy, James A. *Queen's Quarterly*, 41 (Summer 1934), 281-84.

5. Spender, Stephen. *Spectator*, 151 (December 22, 1933), 942.

6. Sutherland, J. R. *Modern Language Review*, 30 (October 1935), 527-28.

7. Walton, Eda Lou. *New York Times Books* (April 1, 1934), p. 10.

8. Williams, Charles. See I-D-97.

9. Wilson, James Southall. *Virginia Quarterly Review*, 10 (July 1934), 475-80.

10. Wilson, T. C. *New Criterion*, 13 (July 1934), 673-75.

11. Initialed: A. N. C. *Saturday Review of Literature*, 10 (March 31, 1934), 596.

12. Unsigned. *Commonweal*, 20 (May 11, 1934), 56.

13. Unsigned. *Notes and Queries*, 165 (December 16, 1933), 431.

14. Unsigned. *Times Literary Supplement* (February 8, 1934), p. 89.

xii. James I (1934) [I-A-vi-2]

1. Dobree, Bonamy. *Spectator*, 153 (September 28, 1934), 443.

2. Pearsall, Robert. *New York Herald Tribune Books* (April 12, 1953), p. 4.

3. Slakey, Roger L. *Catholic World*, 178 (October 1953), 76.

4. Tannenbaum, R. F. *New York Times Books* (April 5, 1953), p. 14.

5. Unsigned. *Times Literary Supplement* (September 20, 1934), p. 629.

xiii. Rochester (1935) [I-A-vi-3]

1. Greene, Graham. *Spectator*, 155 (September 13, 1935), 400-01.

2. Hayward, John. *London Mercury*, 32 (October 1935), 599.

3. Unsigned. *Times Literary Supplement* (September 5, 1935), p. 549.

xiv. Thomas Cranmer of Canterbury (1936) [I-A-iii-5]

1. Jack, Peter Munro. *New York Times Books* (November 15, 1936), p. 39.

2. Unsigned. *Theatre Arts Monthly*, 20 (December 1936), 990.

3. Unsigned. *Times Literary Supplement* (June 20, 1936), p. 512.

xv. Queen Elizabeth (1936) [I-A-vi-4]

1. Unsigned. *Times Literary Supplement* (October 10, 1936), p. 816.

xvi. Descent into Hell (1937) [I-A-ii-6]

1. Burger, Nash. *New York Times Books* (March 21, 1949), p. 21.

xvii. Taliessin through Logres (1938) [I-A-i-6]

1. Unsigned. *Notes and Queries*, 176 (January 6, 1939), 17-18.

2. Unsigned. *Notes and Queries*, 188 (June 30, 1945), 265.

xviii. The Descent of the Dove (1939) [I-A-v-2]

1. Eliot, T. S. *New Statesman and Nation*, 18 (December 9, 1939), 864-65.

2. Harkness, R. E. E. *Christian Century*, 57 (April 3, 1940), 449.

3. Norwood, P. V. *Journal of Religion*, 20 (October 1940), 423.

4. Unsigned. *Times Literary Supplement* (November 11, 1939), p. 652.

xix. The Figure of Beatrice (1943) [I-A-iv-4]

1. Unsigned. *Notes and Queries*, 185 (September 11, 1943), 179.

xx. The Region of the Summer Stars (1944) [I-A-i-7]

1. Humphries, Rolfe. *Nation*, 172 (March 17, 1951), 256.

2. Kreymborg, Alfred. *New York Times Books* (July 22, 1951), p. 12.

3. Nicholl, Louise Townsend. *New York Herald Tribune Books* (February 11, 1951), p. 4.

4. Unsigned. *Notes and Queries*, 188 (March 10, 1945), 109-10.

xxi. All Hallows' Eve (1945) [I-A-ii-7]

1. Bower, Anthony. *Nation*, 167 (November 13, 1948), 551.

2. Farrelly, John. *New Republic*, 119 (November 8, 1948), 25.

3. Graham, Dorothy. *Catholic World*, 168 (December 1948), 252-53.

4. McLaughlin, Richard. *Saturday Review of Literature*, 31 (October 23, 1948), 16-17, 28.

5. Stewart, John L. *Sewanee Review*, 57 (Spring 1949), 307-17.

6. Sugrue, Thomas. *New York Herald Tribune Books* (October 11, 1948), p. 11.

7. Walsh, Chad. *New York Times Books* (October 17, 1948), p. 47.

8. Unsigned. *Atlantic Monthly*, 183 (January 1949), 89.

xxii. The House of the Octopus (1945) [I-A-iii-7]

1. Ridler, Anne. *Poetry London*, 3 (September/October 1947), 49-50.

xxiii. Arthurian Torso (1948) [I-A-iv-5]

1. Daniel, Glyn E. *Cambridge Journal*, 3 (1950), 382.

2. Housman, John E. *Review of English Studies*, 1 (January 1950), 84-85.

3. Mahood, M. M. *Modern Language Review*, 45 (April 1950), 238-39.

4. Mathew, Gervase. *Time and Tide*, 30 (January 1, 1949), 14.

xxiv. The Image of the City (1958) [I-A-iv-6]

1. Dawson, Lawrence R. *Commonweal*, 69 (March 27, 1959), 671-72.

2. Jones, John. *New Statesman and Nation*, 56 (December 27, 1958), 914-15.

3. Robson, W. W. *Spectator*, 201 (December 5, 1958), 835.

4. Winter, Gibson. *Christian Century*, 76 (July 22, 1959), 853.

D. Dissertations

(Previously listed in § II-B; original numbers from that section retained)

10. Bolling, Douglas Townshend. "Three Romances by Charles Williams." University of Iowa, 1970. *Dissertation Abstracts*, 31 (1971), 4755A.

20. Chandler, John Herrick. "Charles Williams, the Poet of the Co-Inherence." University of Chicago, 1964.

31. Dawson, Lawrence Russell. "Charles Williams as Reviewer and Reviewed." University of Michigan, 1960. *Dissertation Abstracts*, 20 (1960), 4659.

35. Dowie, William John, Jr. "Religious Fiction in a Profane Time: Charles Williams, C. S. Lewis and J. R. R. Tolkien." Brandeis, 1970. *Dissertation Abstracts*, 31 (1970), 2911A.

51. Fullman, Christopher Edward. "The Mind and Art of Charles Williams: A Study of His Poetry, Plays, the Novels." University of Wisconsin, 1955.

54. Gigrich, John P. "An Immortality for Its Own Sake: A Study of the Concept of Poetry in the Writings of Charles Williams." Catholic University, Washington, 1953.

76. Hines, Joyce R. "Getting Home: A Study of Fantasy and the Spiritual Journey in the Christian Supernatural Novels of Charles Williams and George MacDonald." C.U.N.Y., 1972.

Dissertation Abstracts International, 33 (August 1972), 755-756A.

77. Howard, Thomas T. "Charles Williams' Experiment in the Novel." New York University, 1970. *Dissertation Abstracts*, 31 (1970), 1760A.

80. Ingraham, Vernon Leland. "The Verse Drama of Charles Williams." University of Pennsylvania, 1965. *Dissertation Abstracts*, 26 (1966), 7318.

104. Mello Moser, Fernando de. "Charles Williams: Demanda, visão e mito." Gráfico Santelmo, Lisboa, 1969.

121. Peckham, Robert Wilson. "The Novels of Charles Williams." University of Notre Dame, 1965.

130. Reilly, Robert J. "Romantic Religion in the Work of Owen Barfield, C. S. Lewis, Charles Williams, and J. R. R. Tolkien." Michigan State University, 1960. *Dissertation Abstracts*, 21 (1960), 3461-62.

132. Roulet, William Matthew. "The Figure of the Poet in the Arthurian Poems of Charles Williams." St. John's University, 1965. *Dissertation Abstracts*, 28 (1965), 2694A.

134. Russell, Mariann Barbara. "The Idea of the City of God." Columbia University, 1965. *Dissertation Abstracts*, 26 (1965), 3350-3351A.

157. Thrash, Lois Glenn. "Thematic Use of the Characters in the Novels of Charles Williams." Texas Tech University, 1972. *Dissertation Abstracts*, 33 (1972), 4436A.

159. Trowbridge, Clinton W. "The Twentieth Century British Supernatural Novel." University of Florida, 1958. *Dissertation Abstracts*, 18 (1960), 1800.

176. Wright, Marjorie Evelyn. "The Cosmic Kingdom of Myth: A Study in the Myth-Philosophy of Charles Williams, C. S. Lewis, and J. R. R. Tolkien." University of Illinois, 1960. *Dissertation Abstracts*, 21 (1960), 3464-65.

180. Zylstra, Sape Anne. "Charles Williams: An Analysis and Appraisal of His Major Work." Emory University, 1969. *Dissertation Abstracts*, 30 (1969), 4468A.

III. Indexes

A. Index of Names

Abercrombie, Lascelles. I-A-iv-1; I-B-11, 12.
Adams, Robert Martin. II-B-1.
Agee, James. II-B-91.
Alexander (the Great). I-A-vi-6.
Allan, Jim. II-B-2.
Allot, Kenneth. I-B-26; II-B-3.
Amis, Kingsley. II-B-4.
Arns, Karl. II-C-i-8; II-C-vii-1.
Arrowsmith, J. E. S. II-C-v-1.
Auden, W. H. I-A-V-2; II-B-3, 6, 7, 8, 45.

Barfield, Owen. II-B-89, 129, 130.
Batho, Edith C. II-C-xi-1.
Baugh, Albert C. II-B-98.
Beaumont, Ernest. II-B-9.
Blake, William. I-C-39.
Blunden, Edmund. I-A-iv-1.
Bolles, Edwin C. II-B-98.
Bolling, Douglas Townshend. II-B-10.
Borrow, Anthony. II-B-11.
Bower, Anthony. II-C-xxi-1.
Bradby, Anne. I-C-17, 18.
Braude, Nan. II-B-12, 13.
Breit, Harvey. II-C-iv-1.
Bridges, Robert. I-A-iv-1; I-C-9, 14; II-B-79.
Brown, Robert McAfee. II-B-14.
Browning, Robert. I-E-5.
Burger, Nash. II-C-xvi-1.
Burnham, Philip. II-C-ix-1.

B.   Index of Titles of Williams's Works

(Alphabetized with omission of initial *A, An,* and *The*)

General Categories

Poetry   I-A-i
Novels   I-A-ii
Plays   I-A-iii
Criticism   I-A-iv
Theology   I-A-v

Biographies   I-A-vi
Poems, Stories   I-B
Articles, Letters   I-C
Reviews   I-D
Edited Works   I-E

"Absence." I-B-4.
All Hallows' Eve. I-A-ii-7; II-B-9, 21, 29, 48, 102, 119, 143, 150, 158; reviews, II-C-xxi.
"Antichrist and the City's Laws." I-C-24.
"Apologue on the Parable of the Wedding Garment." I-B-18.
Arthurian Torso. I-A-i-7; I-A-iv-5; II-B-83, 94, 120, 132; reviews, II-C-xxiii.
"Autocriticism." I-C-12.

Bacon. I-A-vi-1; reviews, II-C-x.
"Ballade of a Street Door." I-B-30.
"Beauty Lately." I-B-6.
"Blake and Wordsworth." I-C-39.
A Book of Victorian Narrative Verse. I-E-2.
"Briseis." I-B-2.
"Byron and Byronism." I-C-22.

"The Calling of Arthur." I-B-15, 26.
"The Carol of Amen House." I-B-9.

"Charles Williams on *Taliessin through Logres.*" I-C-38.
The Chaste Wanton. I-A-iii-4.

C. Index of Titles of Works about Williams

(Alphabetized with omission of initial *A, An,* and *The*.)

"The Impact of Charles Williams' Death on C. S. Lewis."
II-B-84.
"Impact on America." II-B-53.
"The Inklings and the Myth." II-B-128.
Introduction to Charles Williams. II-A-1.
Introduction to *Image of the City and Other Essays*.
II-B-131.
Introduction to *James I* by Charles Williams. II-B-141.
Introduction to "The Noises That Weren't There"
by Charles Williams. II-B-135.
Introduction to *The Protestant Mystics*. II-B-7.

"King Arthur and the Grail in the Poetry of Charles
Williams." II-B-55.
*King Arthur Today: The Arthurian Legend in English and
American Literature, 1901-1953.* II-B-155.
Lebende Antike: Symposion für Rudolf Sühnel. II-B-55.
Letters of C. S. Lewis. II-B-95.
Letters of James Agee to Father Flye. II-B-91.
Light on C. S. Lewis. II-B-53.
"Lines on the Reverend's Black Beard, Begun 29
June Anno Domini 1965 at the Request of His
Lady-Love." II-B-5.
"Love and Rejection in Charles Williams." II-B-16.

*Man in Modern Fiction: Some Minority Opinions on
Contemporary American Writing.* II-B-49.
"Many Dimensions: The Images of Charles
Williams." II-B-47.
"The Martyr as Dramatic Hero." II-B-8.
"The Mathematics of the Soul." II-B-34.
*Milton: The Modern Phase: A Study of Twentieth-Century
Criticism.* II-B-111.
"The Mind and Art of Charles Williams: A Study of His
Poetry, Plays, the Novels." II-B-51.